ALICE
MILLER

From
Rage to Courage

Answers to Readers' Letters

For information about permission to reproduce selections from this book,
write to Permissions, W. W. Norton & Company, Inc., 500 Fifth Avenue,
New York, NY 10110

For information about special discounts for bulk purchases, please contact
W. W. Norton & Company, Inc., Special Sales at specialsales@wwnorton.com
or 800–233–4830

Manufacturing by Courier Westford
Book design by Molly Heron
Production manager: Devon Zahn

Library of Congress Cataloging-in-Publication Data
Miller, Alice.
From rage to courage : answers to readers' letters / Alice Miller.—1st ed.
          p. cm.
ISBN 978-0-393-33789-1 (pbk.)
1. Child abuse—Psychological aspects. 2. Adult child abuse victims—
Mental health. 3. Abused children—Mental health. I Title.
RC569.5.C55M5554 2009
616.85'822390651—dc22

                                                 2009020632

W. W. Norton & Company, Inc.
500 Fifth Avenue, New York, NY 10110
www.wwnorton.com

W. W. Norton & Company, Ltd.
Castle House, 75/76 Wells Street,
London WIT 3QT

1 2 3 4 5 6 7 8 9 0

Preface

I HAVE DECIDED TO publish these answers in book form because there are still people who have no access to the Internet. But even those who can read these responses online may find it more convenient to own the book for quick reference when they are looking for a particular passage. A degree of computer literacy is necessary, however, for those who wish to read the original letters.

When I was young, I was an avid reader of Sigmund Freud. But I lost my interest in psychoanalysis when I started working with patients. I found that the concepts and theories I had been confronted with during my psychoanalytical training were an invitation to blame individuals themselves for their distress. Those theories were in fact designed to "repair" them or "put them straight." In this approach I detected elements of the disastrous and highly abusive ideal of education and upbringing known in German as *schwarze Pädagogik* ("poisonous pedagogy").

What interested me was how this distress had come about, the childhood factors that might explain the sufferings of these adults, and the ways in which they might be able to free themselves from the severe consequences of cruel parenting. None of the theories I came across seemed genuinely willing to engage with childhood reality, and this put them fully in line with the attitude of society in general.

It was my patients themselves who provided indirect answers to my questions. Their reports on what they had been through in childhood revealed facts that had hardly ever been addressed during my training: the severe cruelty inflicted on children by their own parents.

At the same time, I became aware of my patients' deeply entrenched resistance to remembering these painful events: they were extremely reluctant to feel the tragic situation they had been in as children and to take it seriously. Some of them described acts of monstrous cruelty with a complete lack of emotion, as if they were something that was only to be expected. They believed their parents had loved them and that as children they had richly deserved severe punishment because they were so insufferable. The regularity with which true feelings were denied or split off made me realize that almost all of us tend to deny, or at least play down, the pain caused by the injuries we suffered in childhood. We do this because we still fear punishment at the hands of our parents, who could not bear to accept us as we truly were. These childhood fears live on in the adult. If they remain unconscious, that is if they are not identified as such, then they will retain their virulence to the end of our lives. Unfortunately, these fears also live on in those who advance theories that camouflage childhood reality and that concentrate instead on the nature of "psychic structures." This approach began with Freud and was later taken over by C. G. Jung and others. Like present-day "spiritualist" interpretations, these theories all served one purpose: to allay the fears of the maltreated children these therapists still were.

As almost everyone on this planet received beatings when they were small and do their best to repress the fear of punishment at the hands of their parents, it is difficult to make this unconscious dynamic apparent. After all, no one wants to be told about sufferings they have been fighting to suppress for decades, sometimes sacrificing their health in the process. After listening to the tragic stories of my patients for twenty years without letting myself be confused by the theories of Freud and others, I wrote *The Drama of the Gifted Child*, in which I pointed the finger at facts that almost everyone knows but strongly denies. Subsequently, I published *For Your Own Good*, referring to three biographies to indicate the social consequences that cruel parenting can have. One of the things the book revealed was the way in which the complete and utter eradication of empathy from the earliest years and constant persecution by the father turned the former child Adolf Hitler into a mass murderer with the blood of millions of people on his hands. In my later books I have repeatedly demonstrated how the political careers of mass murderers like Stalin, Saddam Hussein, Slobodan Milošević, and others were rooted in the denial of the humiliations inflicted on them in childhood.

I received a great deal of praise for my investigations, and yet no one followed in my footsteps. Why? Presumably because almost all of us are victims of more or less severe cruelty, but this is something we either cannot or will not acknowledge until we have finally faced up to the fact.

Naturally I cannot prove this hypothesis because I cannot investigate the lives of all the people in the world. But the letters addressed to my Web site in the last few years reveal the reality of childhood abuse in a way that can hardly be denied. The authors of those letters have decided to break their unconscious vow of silence *despite* their understandable fear. Encouraged by my books and articles, they have attempted to unearth the memories of their early childhood years, to admit to their true feelings, and to take seriously their indignation, anger, and rage at the behavior of their parents. They were astonished that instead of being punished for this they achieved much greater freedom by recalling those memories. Suddenly they were able to understand the course of their own lives much better and to revive their lost empathy for the children they once were. In this way they learned something they were never allowed to learn as children: to take their own pain, and other feelings, seriously. One reader wrote to me recently: "When I was small, I once fell off a wall. An adult passing by asked me if I had hurt myself. I shall never forget it because it was the first time in my childhood that anyone had ever asked me that question. For my parents, my pain and my sorrows just never existed, so I had to wipe them out too."

The man used this example to illustrate the entire atmosphere of his childhood, something we have to discover in order to free ourselves of it and the consequences it has had. This goes well beyond the active engagement with individual traumas that present-day trauma therapy sets out to induce. It is the discovery of years of unremitting captivity, a discovery achieved by finally owning up to our feelings. That captivity was a time defined by indifference, lack of understanding, refusal of contact, cruelty, sadism, deceit, lies, and very often perversion.

The contents of these letters are by no means exceptional. Millions of people have shared the same fate, but this fact has been concealed (so far) by their silence, their inability or reluctance to put their sufferings into words. So the writers of the letters I answer here are pioneers. They are exceptional because they have dared to overcome the fear of their parents, because they have had the courage to admit to their own truth. I can no longer ask them for their permission to publish their letters in book form, but those letters can be found on my Web site. My answers show how I have attempted to accompany these people in their quest for their own selves.

Very severe cruelty in childhood is hardly ever recognized as such. Usually, it is considered part of quite normal upbringing. The extreme—often total—denial of the pain we have suffered not only thwarts recognition of the wrongs done to us. Above all, it negates the anger of the little child that has to be suppressed in the body for fear of punishment. Parents are honored out of fear, and the adult child waits a whole lifetime for their insight and love, thus remaining trapped in a form of attachment sustained by the fear of being abandoned. The consequences of attachments that are dependent on the absence of true feelings are mental and physical disorders and the suppression and sacrifice of life satisfaction and happiness.

These answers to the question posed to me by my readers show how they have attempted to find the way to their own truth. Initially they recognize the lifelong denial of their reality and sense for the first time the pent-up though justified anger caused by the threats they were exposed to—beatings, humiliation, deceit, rejection, confusion, neglect, and exploitation. But if they manage to sense their anger and grief at what they have missed out on in life, almost all of them rediscover the alert, inquisitive child who never had the slightest chance of being perceived, respected, and listened to by the parents. Only then will the adult give the child this respect, because he or she knows the true story and can thus learn to understand and love the child within.

To their great surprise, the symptoms that have tormented them all their lives gradually disappear. Those symptoms were the price they had to pay for the denial of reality caused by awe of their parents.

Unquestioning adulation of parents and ancestors, regardless of what they have done, is required not only by some religions but by *all* of them, without exception, although the adult children frequently have to pay for this self-denial with severe illness symptoms. The reason why this is the case is not difficult to identify, though it is rarely taken into account. Children are forced to ignore their need for respect and are not allowed to express it, so they later look to their own children to gratify that need. This is the origin of the Fourth/Fifth Commandment ("honor your father and mother").

This intrinsic dynamic is observable in all religions. Religions were obviously created not by people respected in childhood but by adults starved of respect from childhood on and brought up to obey their parents unswervingly. They have learned to live with the compulsive self-deception forced on them in their earlier years. Many impressive rituals have been devised to make children ignore their true feelings and accept the cruelties of their parents without demur. They are forced to suppress their anger, their *true* feelings, and honor parents who do not deserve such reverential treatment, otherwise they will be doomed to intolerable feelings of guilt all their lives. Luckily, there are now individuals who are beginning to desist from such self-mutilation and to resist the attempt to instill guilt feelings into them. These people are standing up against a practice that its proponents have always considered ethical. In fact, however, it is profoundly unethical because it produces illness and hinders healing. It flies in the face of the laws of life.

From
Rage to Courage

I

FROM JULY TO DECEMBER

2005

27 ⌇ *The Pattern of a Lie*

You tell us in your letter that your father abused you sexually when you were three years old and that he abandoned you at the age of eight because you did not love or appreciate him. He then e-mailed you many years later explaining that he had abandoned you out of love so that you would be protected. You are now twenty-three years old, suffer many symptoms, and report the "amazing" compulsion to abandon people who love you and care about you. You write that you do this because you feel "that the other person had been better off" without you. In this way, you try to make sense of a perversion so that you can believe you were loved, because every child absolutely needs to be loved. But the body of the intelligent twenty-three-year-old woman feels the truth and rebels against the lie. It cannot recover as long as the adult clings to the illusion that her father loved her. A father who exploits the body of his three-year-old daughter is a criminal who is incapable of love. In addition, he conceals the crime by telling her that he loved her. Your letter shows that the adult daughter does want to know her truth and that she will thus eventually get it. Reading my last articles and the last interview for *ONA* [a Slovenian periodical] on the Web site may be helpful on this path. But now, by repeating the pattern of your father (I make you suffer "for your own good"), you protect your father, you deny his lies and perversions, and your body screams for its truth.

AUGUST 2005

15 ❧ To Be a Hostage

I am glad that you mentioned the Stockholm syndrome. It is absolutely the same mechanism that works for an abused child. The Stockholm syndrome was discovered after a bank robbery during which hostages were held for almost a whole week. Now, imagine being under constant terror for many years. The consequences of having been a hostage as a child are more serious and lingering because the fear of a mortal danger was inflicted at a time when the brain of the child has not yet been structured.

Beaten children are not allowed to defend themselves. In order to make sense of what happens, they feel guilty, they feel that they deserve the beatings. In order to survive they must deny the endured brutality, suppress their rage, and believe that they are bad. As grown-ups, they don't even know that they survived terror, as they will tell you: I have been spanked but this didn't kill me. They learn early to believe in lies and they continue to live with these lies and produce new generations of unconscious people. They say: The Bible tells us we should not spare the rod and the child must learn the difference between right and wrong. The truth is that the child learns the wrong lesson, that spanking is harmless; but spanking children is the most brutal crime, because it kills in the children the capacity to think, to feel, and to have empathy with themselves and others.

SEPTEMBER 2005

9 ৎ *The Body Never Lies*

You write: "I used to have beautiful hair and a couple of times, certainly not more, my mother dragged me by it around the dining room table. It was a fear of mine, but did not happen more than twice (was it not enough to fear the mother for one's whole life?). However, I do not see the links and my mind is going round in circles with this." Your body gives you the answer but you refuse to listen. It reminds you of your mother's cruelty, but you are afraid to feel the rage, you are afraid that she could drag you by your beautiful hair again. Now, she can't. The body only wants to help you. I hope that one day you will listen to it.

18 ৎ *"Moderately Violent"*

Your story is heartbreaking but not at all exceptional; I have been receiving letters like yours since I published *The Drama of the Gifted Child* twenty-six years ago. In all these letters the mother is called "moderately violent," while the facts described an extreme horror. I hope that my recent book *The Body Never Lies* can help you to take care of the terribly mistreated small girl you once were. If your mother loved you, she would not have been able to mistreat you so cruelly nor to wish you to destroy yourself by taking drugs.

19 ⌘ *Abuse at the Workplace*

I think that reading two books written by Marie-France Hirigoyen (about stalking the soul and stalking in the workplace) could be very helpful to you. Also, if your therapist could enable you to feel (not only understand intellectually) how it was for you as a small child to live for years with your abusive parents. If you never acknowledged these strong feelings, maybe you are experiencing them now in the workplace without understanding the source of their intensity. By knowing emotionally what your body is telling you, you will slowly overcome the effects of early endured abuse.

20 ⌘ *Spanking Abuse?*

To spank a child is a despiteful and dirty act because it involves a powerless person who is not allowed to defend her- or himself nor to escape from the aggression and ignorance of the spanker. It is also the most destructive act because it damages the brain of the victims, who will repeat for their whole lives the lies and feeblemindedness of King Solomon: spare the rod, spoil the child. Exactly the opposite is true: the rod spoils the child and leaves lingering effects for a lifetime. Solomon learned his lie from his own parents as you did from yours, as your children will learn it from you.

OCTOBER 2005

7 ❧ Violence Against Children Produces Violent Adults

I am glad that you have read some of my books and want to help others to understand what happens to them. It is not an easy job but a very necessary one. I think that understanding the dynamic of violence makes every responsible leader want to share that knowledge with others. Violence against children produces violent adults. This obvious truth is, however, totally denied because almost everyone was a victim of child abuse and doesn't want to acknowledge it. So they continue to fool each other: in philosophy, literature, religion. But their bodies don't let themselves be fooled. They continue to reproduce their stories and so the abuse continues. It is thus time for our mind to understand what happens, to leave the darkness, and to stop the abuse. Preaching virtue is totally ineffective as long as religions forbid emotional honesty. However, this is exactly what *all of them* continue to do. My book *The Body Never Lies* makes that clear for everybody who wants to know.

25 ❧ Blindness for the Crimes of Parents Can Be Found in All Ethnic Groups

I think that it takes much courage to gain the emotional honesty and awareness that your letter shows. It is true that black people have suffered so much from the cruelty of white people that the solidarity with their families probably gave them a kind of protection. But there is no less blindness to the crimes of parents among other ethnic groups. It is the same all over the world, among Europeans, Chinese, Japanese, Christians, Muslims. In all religions it is forbidden to have authentic feelings, to feel rage toward the abusers; it is instead allowed to take revenge on small children, to beat them, and to teach them the lie that cruelty is "for their own good." Most of these children believe later as adults in the benefit of beatings and don't know that they are stuck forever in the fear of their parents. They remain scared children their entire lives instead of becoming adults who can be respectful of their offspring. Concerning Prozac and other medications, I think that they may help us to feel better for a while but can block the experience of emotions stored up in our body. However, it is exactly these emotions that give us access to our history so that we can heal.

26 ᴄ The Healing Potential of Rage and Anger

When I wrote The Drama of the Gifted Child in 1978, I didn't yet fully recognize the healing potential of rage and anger. In my opinion today, it is not enough for a former mistreated child to grieve about what happened, as psychoanalysts assume. It is indispensable to rebel against the endured cruelty, to clearly recognize and reject it. Only this way can we become free of the tendency to unconsciously repeat the same pattern with our children. The suppressed rage will exist in our bodies if it is never consciously experienced or expressed.

NOVEMBER 2005

2 & *A Murderer Cannot Feel*

Your letter shows that thanks to my book *For Your Own Good* you know almost everything you need to understand and to describe the dynamics of a serial crime. Why are you, though, hesitating to do what you want to do and to write down what you have learned? Everything is clearly confirmed by every detail of your story. Are you, perhaps, waiting for the confirmation of the murderer himself? He is the last person who can give it to you.

Murderers don't know why they act in the way they do because their feelings are totally blocked. They have no orientation and no understanding of themselves. This is why they are unable to tell you right away: "I go on to kill again and again, to take revenge for what has been done to me, for all these numerous mutilations of my integrity, humiliations, attempts to murder me—all mistreatments and soul-murders I once had to endure."

If murderers could speak like that, if they were emotionally, deeply aware of how they became criminals, if they could *feel the pain about their damaged lives*, they would be unable to kill anybody. It is exactly the *repressed* rage and pain, the total lack of authentic feelings, that drive them to destruction. The same is valid for tyrants like Hitler and Stalin. The "bad seed" theory explains not only the desire to abuse; it also reveals the blindness stemming from past abuse. Consciously experienced feelings, even feelings of extreme rage, never result in crimes.

If you want to understand more about the destructive power of repressed emotions, you can read my books *Banished Knowledge* and *Breaking Down the Wall of Silence*. The examples you will find there will give you the background and the evidence of my state-ment: *There is no other reason for serial crimes than the repression and denial of pain endured in an extremely cruel childhood.*

Of course, criminality is not the only consequence of avoiding old pain. There are plenty of others as well: addictions, prostitu-tion, psychic illnesses, war, etc. The denial of childhood injuries is shared by the whole society, therapists included. You can easily recognize it everywhere once you succeed in acknowledging your own denial.

DECEMBER 2005

4 ❧ *The Crime of Not Protecting*

Your siblings did to you what they learned from your parents, whom you still protect because you are so afraid of them. But by saying this I don't want to minimize the suffering that you endured at the hands of your sister and brother. It must have been terrible. Your rage, however, seems to be more free when you talk about them. It is only totally blocked when you think of your parents, who still laugh at you when you try to complain.

5 ❧ *No Longer in the Trap*

You got it. Your success doesn't surprise me. You may still experi-ence pain, fear, and anger, even much anger. But now you will know *why* these emotions come up, what they have to tell you, if you want to understand them. You are no longer in the trap from which most people never escape of waiting for parents to change, of keeping illusions alive and paying for this self-betrayal with chronic illnesses. Now, nobody can take your knowledge and your new experiences away. They will lead you. Since you dare to love yourself, to listen to yourself, you will dare to listen to your patients too. From their childhood history you will learn everything you need to be able to help them. Theories and medication serve only to support our own denial. Once we can move past that, we regain empathy as you describe it. The more you give up your illusions, the more you will feel who you really are.

6 ᴗ *Forgiveness Is a Cover*

Yes, you are right, forgiveness is a cover. It will "get you back to where you started" and will not help your mother either. Only she can help herself if she is ready to feel the pain (this is possible at every age). Try to feel the child you once were and don't ignore his suffering. Stay with him now and explain to him that your mother's letter doesn't change anything about what happened then, what he had to endure alone, without any helping witness, for such a long time. Be this witness for him; do not put new burdens like forgiveness on him. They would block your work again.

18 ᴗ *"I Can't Honor You"*

Your rabbis may be right, as far as the theory is concerned: God is perfect, man is not. The commandment comes from God, but parents are human and their failures are understandable (one may ask: Are mistakes also understandable if children make them, or must children be punished by beatings when they show that they are not perfect? Should parents also be beaten for their imperfection? Why not?) I wonder if you have already tried to use these theories in a concrete case. Could you, for instance, tell your parents: "I can't honor you because when I was small and helpless you humiliated me by spanking and slapping me, you implanted fear and rage in my small body that caused me later panic attacks from which I am still suffering"? Can you imagine speaking in this way with your parents? What kind of reaction do you expect from your parents if you say the truth, that you cannot honor them? Loving understanding and apologies, or rage and indignation in the name of God? I assume that your body knows very well why it produces panic attacks. All religious families who spank their children are not only cruel but also highly confusing, because they pretend to do it in the name of God. In this way they betray the children's confidence, because these children will believe their whole lives what they so early had to believe. Judaism is not an exception. You will hear the same theories from the clergy of other religions. But none of them tackles the concrete fact that slapping and beating a small child is cruel, humiliating, and damaging to their brains, especially if it happens to a child before the age of three years old when the brain is being structured. Religious leaders seem not to know (or not to care) that spanking and slapping children makes them violent or chronically scared, often for their whole lives. Above all, it teaches them to stay ignorant and to teach their own children the same absurdities they learned from their parents: that *God needs their suffering.* You write that you are Orthodox. In my opinion orthodoxy is not about love, it is about obedience. Thus you may hate what I have written here. But I wrote it to the person who has panic attacks, who wants to know her true feelings, who tries to understand their meaning and wants to be honest, even if that means not being obedient.

19 ❧ Listen to Your Client's History

If you are interested in diagnosis, go to a library and look for the books. If you are interested in your client's history, listen to her and she will tell you what you both need to learn: the facts.

22 ❧ Thanks for the Epiphany!

You say that you are not interested in your childhood and you share this attitude with most people. But not many have in themselves a child who so strongly forces them to look to the past. Your child does it in a brilliant way, creating dreams that can hardly be mis-understood and seems to do it at any cost; it doesn't give up until you are ready to go to the "other" rooms and leave the prison. Once you are ready to do it, to feel and understand the pain and the extreme suffering of the child you were, these rooms will become less and less spooky and awkward; they will make more and more sense and will no longer bother you at night. If you are going to take this path with the help of a therapist, my FAQ list at the Web site may be helpful in looking for a good informed witness. Also my last book, *The Body Never Lies*, as well as articles and interviews on the Web site, can serve as your witnesses.

26 ❧ We Pay Our Loyalty to Our Parents with Our Depressions

You might be right, in some cases: when the parents are still alive and can show themselves (sometimes?) as kind, friendly, charming, it seems "that hope indeed springs eternal and this can be very painful at times." However, I don't agree with you that depression is unavoidable, even when the parents are alive. I wonder if you have read my recent book, *The Body Never Lies*. A better title would probably have been *You Can't Fool Your Body*. The problem is that in the eternal search for love from our parents, most of us can't give up the illusion that once, just now, at this moment perhaps, they will finally become loving. With this illusion we are in danger of betraying our bodies and the memory of the child. Because the body knows the history of the child we once were, it knows of the cruelty the child had to endure without feeling it, because it was too dangerous. Now, as an adult, you could feel the pain of the small, teased child of two successful parents if you had access to his suffering. But maybe your still-idealized image of your parents hinders you in getting this access. Ask the child inside you how they treated you when you were small, helpless, so totally dependent on their love. Were you never spanked or slapped? Do you know how it feels? It is not necessary to fall again and again into the state of depression, but protecting our parents from rage of the once-beaten, humiliated child blocks our feelings and thus produces depression. Try to imagine what you would have felt if somebody had told you in your childhood that beating children is a crime (as it actually is). And if your parents are able to tease you now, try to imagine why they did the same to the defenseless child you once were. If you can feel the rage, the fear, and the sorrow, and if you dare to see the cruelty you had to endure silently without helping witnesses, your depression *will* disappear. Because by discovering and understanding the pain of the former neglected child, you start to love and cherish him, perhaps for the first time in your life. Usually, parents are less violent at seventy than at thirty. If a client succeeds in his or her therapy to see their parents of *then* (not of today) and to feel the fear their body remembers, they will no longer suffer from panic attacks or addictions. But as long as we are compelled to protect our parents, we pay our loyalty with depressions.

27 ℰ *The Adult Can Try to Feel*

You are absolutely right: it is your body that knows everything you need to know, and analytical interpretations will only help you to build up new illusions. Everything you write makes sense to me. If the child was not allowed to see and say the truth, it is not surprising that the adult prefers to be depressed rather than to feel the rage, because the rage could bring the child into mortal danger. But the adult can try to feel, not everything all together, but step by step. And you have the courage to try.

31 ℰ *The Courage to See and to Feel*

The child you once were, the child living in your body, will become less alone than he was before, when you didn't know anything about how you had been made "happy" and obedient. Now, as you become more and more aware of what happened to you, how cruelly you were treated, and as you begin to feel empathy for this silenced child, you start to love him, to protect him and to explain to him that knowledge is not a mortal danger. On the contrary, it will help you, the adult and the child, to leave the prison of denial and blindness. I wish you the courage to see and to feel. It is all you need.

II

FROM JANUARY
TO DECEMBER

2006

JANUARY 2006

1 ₰ *Therapists Afraid of Questioning Parents*

I obviously idealized your country. In my book *The Body Never Lies* you will find many examples of how therapists all over the world are afraid of questioning the behavior of parents. The problem is that the more people were abused the more they defend their parents because the fear of the small, defenseless, severely offended child is still very active in them. It holds them in a state of dependency and denial that often causes panic attacks in adulthood.

9 ₰ *The Child Has No Choice*

For staying silent, victims often pay with depression, then they take antidepressants, and then they take something against the secondary effects of antidepressants, and so on and on. Staying silent is rarely a must; it is a choice, at least for adults. Only children have no choice, and their fear unfortunately stays with many of them their entire lives, meaning that they don't take the risk and never experience how relieving it can be to speak out.

9 ⸱ *Antidepressants Suppress Your Truth*

You write: "Meanwhile, I've had a headache for seven months; I have the impression of being constantly dizzy; my blood pressure can fall severely. I am taking antidepressants and twice a week I go to psychotherapy. I love my parents, who worry about me. . . . My nightly dreams are essentially scenes where I get furious toward a bunch of people from my environment (I beat my sister, break dishes, set my colleague on fire, etc.). I would like very much to stop taking the medication, but I am extremely scared that my situation is irreversible. Your book is helping me to believe that this condition is temporary and that I will succeed in becoming healthy by regaining my feelings, which are repressed because of my childhood."

The depression proves that you are suppressing your strongest feelings. By taking antidepressants you are also suppressing your truth. You love your parents but at night you experience rage— which fortunately you still can feel. I hope that your therapist can help you to understand who deserves your rage and why. When your child, who had to suffer cruelty, feels accompanied by a courageous witness, you will no longer need medication and will be able to feel and understand the origins of your suffering.

10 ⸱ *Tumors Are the Screams of*
Silent Children

I don't think that your patients need psychology or psychiatric help, since they would reject it anyway. In no way do they need psychoanalytical theories. What they doubtlessly need is to come in contact with their emotions, with the history of their childhood and the tragedies connected to it. They have denied them their whole lives. Thanks to your compassion (see my article on "Indignation" and other articles on the Web site) they may dare to give up their denial, and I would not be surprised if their tumors decreased. These tumors are the screams of the silent children who never rebelled against the cruelty they endured in childhood and who are now asking the adult to finally stop denying the truth. I wish you success in your endeavors and hope that you can forget the psychoanalytic theories that would only conceal your view of your patients' childhood reality.

12 ❧ The Suffering of Children

I was very moved by your thoughts concerning Schiller and agree with you that, thanks to the first four years of life spent with his loving mother, he might have had the potential to understand the meaning of his rebellions in *Wilhelm Tell* and the other dramas. But in his time the presence of an enlightened witness was unthinkable; even today, it is rare. My last book was published in Germany in 2004, but you are the first reader interested in answering the essential question I asked: how can we explain the fact that a man can suffer so much, see so much, and yet have not the slightest inkling that his terrible tragedy has something to do with his suppressed childhood rage? I am glad that you try to enlighten religious people. To me, it is absurd that people imagine a loving God who needs the suffering of children and of his beloved son on the cross. They can imagine this only because they have been told very early that they were spanked to please God.

13 ☙ *How Do I Find My Voice?*

I can imagine that reading my book *The Body Never Lies* could give you some ideas of how you can liberate yourself from guilt and become the loving, protecting parent of the girl you were, so that your inner child will feel taken seriously. The tragedy is that the more the child was mistreated the more the adult she becomes tends to deny this painful fact and to blame herself for the torture. Read also the FAQ list on my Web site if you are looking for a therapist with whom you can learn to *feel* what happened to you and how it hurts.

21 ☙ *Our Body Cannot "Turn the Page"*

Your question is very important, but it contains the assumption that we can manipulate our feelings without letting others pay the price for it. In reality, we cannot. You are saying here what everyone says, what we all have learned from our parents, in school, in church, and even in most of the therapies: "One has to turn the page." It is, without doubt, a nice idea: that the hatred can go away and never ever return. We want to turn the page and live in peace.

Everyone wants this, and it would be nice if it worked. But unfortunately, it does not work. Not at all. Why? Because rage, like all other emotions, cannot be controlled and cannot be manipulated. *It* dictates to us; it forces us to experience it and to understand its causes. It can return every time someone hurts us, and we cannot prevent that, because our body cannot "turn the page"; it demands from us that we listen to it. What we can do, though, is suppress our rage, despite all the consequences: illnesses, addiction, crimes.

When we do not want to feel our justified rage because we already have forgiven our parents even the worst abuses, we will soon find out, to our surprise, that we passed on the same pain we endured to our children or to others. If we are truthful, we will not claim that we acted "for their own good" (that beatings are "a good means of education"). Unfortunately, this is what most parents do say; this is why our society is so hypocritical.

On the "Articles" page on my Web site you can find my text about hatred, which should be able to help you better understand what I am trying to explain. Also the book *The Body Never Lies* can help you to understand more.

22 ⤷ *What I Feel Without Antidepressants*

I thank you for your most important letter, and I congratulate you on having the courage and wisdom to give up the medication and to see what suffering is hidden behind this poison so sought out and appreciated by so many people.

25 ⤷ *Treating Ourselves with Love*

We can't change our past, but we can stop repeating it unconsciously, by denying ourselves love as our parents did. However, we can't achieve this unless we know emotionally what it means for a child to live for years without love, or even surrounded by hatred. If we deny this knowledge, our body will remind us of the work we have to do in order to give the child inside the care and attention she needs now from us.

29 ⸫ Surviving Childhood Corporal Punishment

I hope that many readers of my books will want to exchange their experiences with you. Your action seems to me necessary, especially in your country, where politicians still maintain that there exist "reasonable" beatings, and where they refuse to learn the simplest thing: that the child's brain forms according to its environment. In the first three years of their lives, children learn either violence and brutality or kindness and love.

30 ⸫ A Short Question for Alice

Children never cry without reason. Many times they are not consciously aware of their reasons, but nevertheless crying proves their distress. It is very cruel to leave distressed children alone, for what they most need then is the warm presense of a loving person. Then the source of the trouble can appear in their mind, and they can learn to trust, to express themselves in another, more understandable, way, and screaming is no longer necessary. Screaming should not be seen as bad behavior. It is only a signal of pain.

FEBRUARY 2006

1 ⸫ Hitting Is Not Loving

You are right that hitting is not loving; the assumption that it is is a lie. This lie is still held in high esteem, and children believe what they are told. As adults, they tell their children the same and so we cultivate violence and lies in every new generation. But I don't agree with you when you say that the grandmother *was loving* when she was not hitting the child. It is possible that she was able to play with the child in a way that both of them enjoyed, but this has nothing to do with love. When you love a person, you care about him, you don't want to damage him, to make him suffer, to humiliate him, to destroy his future. A loving person *can't* hit a defenseless child; it is impossible to any decent person to do it. But many don't realize that hitting children is a barbaric habit that excludes every feeling of love.

It is hard to accept that we were not loved at all—but only the truth can really help us.

5 ℮ *Unconscious Hatred*

I think that the first years of his life gave Schiller the sensibility he needed to become aware of the stupidity and cruelty of authoritarian behavior. He described this attitude in his dramas again and again. Most people who don't know anything else don't see it; for them this behavior is normal. In some exceptional cases, if love and honesty were experienced in early childhood, cruelty can later be recognized. This was the case of Schiller; he hated cruelty, hypocrisy, and perversion, but he was unable to consciously hate his own father. The unconscious hatred offended his body; he suffered terribly from corporal pain and died at forty-six.

5 ℮ *Corporal Punishment and Gender*

I think that if we have suffered corporal punishment (and who did not?), we will often be affected by any kind of nonsense people tell us about it. Who can prove "scientifically" which gender is more beaten? What has happened (or still happens?) in British public schools is no longer a secret, I hope, but what happens to small boys and girls in their own homes before they go to school must still be discovered.

7 ❧ The Counseling Profession and Corporal Punishment

Like you, I wonder what can be done to inform people, especially counselors, about the destructive effects of corporal punishment that are so widely denied all over the world. If you read *The Truth Will Set You Free*, you will know that I explain that this universal blindness is caused by the mental barriers we required in early childhood. In my new entry on my Web site, I try to say it more simply. But I must realize that the most active effect of being beaten is actually the fear of the beaten child, which in most cases stays with us our whole lives and forces us to deny the truth. Therapists are no exceptions. Obviously, you have the courage to see and feel what happened to you and maybe you can prepare a book such as you have suggested here. Write and tell us how you would like to present the knowledge you have gained. Perhaps you could write to many different counselors and send them a questionnaire about their opinions on their childhood. Then you could publish the results—without names, of course—to show how the spirit of the poisonous pedagogy remains, still undetected, in the answers. Since the big majority thinks in the same way, you would need to write a comment. You can use my FAQ list on my Web site (see "Articles") as inspiration for your questionnaire if you want to.

9 ౿ *Nurturing Self-Esteem*

To open the eyes of others we must first open our own, by exploring emotionally the atmosphere of our childhood and acknowledging its effects on our adult life. Once we have done this difficult emotional work, plenty of ideas will come up about what we actually want to do.

MARCH 2006

3 ౿ *Effective Therapy*

For me, effective therapy must be able to bring me in touch with the story of the child I was and with her suffering that we usually deny. To bring me to my origins by undoing my denial, I need an enlightened witness who knows his or her history and thus wouldn't be afraid of my own. In my FAQ list I describe how you can find such a therapist. Also, the article "The Longest Path" on my Web site and my book *The Body Never Lies* can be helpful. The therapies you mentioned are mostly not tailored to exploring the histories of childhood except maybe the primal therapy of Arthur Janov. But in my opinion there are some kinds of PT that can be dangerous because their settings produce a dependency on strong feelings and on the person of the therapist and his integrity. You can learn more about this danger if you read the chapter "Helga" in my book *Paths of Life*.

5 & *Forgiveness—Flight from Oneself*

You are by all means right when you ask yourself this question [Am I still carrying a lot of rage?]. You know from your mother that you were beaten very early; you can remember neither the emotional nor the physical pain of the little being that was forced to block out her suffering. But with multiple sclerosis the body can revive these pains if something in the present triggers it (for example, the feeling that no one understands you). If your analyst does not even consider this, try to find a therapist who is not afraid of your history. Maybe my FAQ list on my Web site could help you with this. What your analyst has recommended is in my opinion exactly that which makes us ill, because it suffocates the justifiable rage. The reconciliation can bring some relief for a while because it weakens the agonizing feelings of guilt. One feels like a good, therefore loved, child if one forgives the mistreatments. But the body insists on the truth. I myself tried very hard as a child to understand my parents and have continued these attempts—probably like most analysts—for decades. But this prevented me from discovering the child who was tormented by them. I did not know this child—not in the least. I only knew the suffering of my parents, also of my patients and my friends, but never my own. Only when I gave up trying to understand my parents' childhood (which they themselves did not want to know at all) did it become possible for me to feel the whole extent of my pain and fear. Only then did I discover slowly the history of my childhood and begin to realize my fate. And only then did I lose the physical symptoms that had tried for so long to tell me, in vain, my truth. While I was listening to my patients, I began to understand, through their fates, what happens to beaten children. I comprehended that I betrayed myself. Like so many analysts, I did not know who I truly was, because I was fleeing from myself and believed that I was capable of helping others. Today, I know that I have to understand myself in order to understand others, not the other way around.

7 ⤳ *Trust Your Truth*

You write, "Yours is the only truth I trust." I hope and wish that my books could help you to trust *your* truth, to get in touch with the little girl you once were, to learn to love her in her pain, to give up the distance that separates you from her and from her suffering. She is still waiting for your love—nobody else can replace you.

15 ⤳ *Matriarchy? Patriarchy?*

Thank you for sharing with us your experiences with female teachers and students. I am very sorry that you suffered so much from their cruelty, and I don't doubt even for a moment that things happened in the way you describe them. But I don't think that gender makes a difference when it comes to cruelty. Active cruelty is the effect of endured violence and perversion in childhood and nothing else. Feminists dislike it very much when I write in many books (*The Drama, Banished Knowledge, Breaking Down,* and others) that the space society gives to man to rage and destroy life with impunity is war, whereas for women that space is their home, where they can do whatever they want to their babies and toddlers to teach them to obey. What they do in this way—never controlled, never punished—is to cripple millions of people who will never accuse them of their crimes because almost every child loves his or her mother and would never, never get her in trouble. They may hate the whole world or all women, but their own mother must stay protected from their hatred forever. In this way we revolve in a vicious circle of blindness. A brutally beaten child will, as an adult, prefer becoming a serial killer to accusing his mother of brutality. And the same is true for crazy dictators who become "heroes" for whole nations because people learn so early to love and admire the people who were cruel to them—no matter what they really did.

19 ౬ The Causes of Addiction

You write that you have read my last book and at the same time you write, "As an addict I would love to fix myself with a pill and be normal." There are many pills that promise you such an outcome, so why do you write to me? If you read my book, you must know that I do not have this kind of pill to sell and that I insist on the fact that all psychic disturbances and addictions have their causes in the denial of one's own childhood's suffering. That suffering must be found and respected in therapy with an enlightened witness.

20 ౬ Buddhism and Your Work

If you found peace in the Buddhist philosophy, that's okay. But then why do you need my confirmation? I can only say that I don't know of any Buddhist who said or has written that hitting children is a crime and the cause of human misery. Do you know of such an author?

20 ⚷ How to Respond to Bullying and Mobbing?

Do you know the book *Stalking the Soul* by Marie-France Hirigoyen? She is an expert in what you are looking for; she has the courage to see through lies and she also knows my books. I suggest that you arrange an interview with her (she lives in Paris). If you want to publish anything on child abuse, you can copy articles or interviews already published on my Web site.

22 ⚷ The Absurdity of the Belief That Hitting Children Is Harmless

Absurdity seems to be the most beloved food of all humanity (not only in our culture). All over the world people believe that hitting children is harmless. We can't change these people, but we can do our best to inform them, as you did.

26 ⚷ The Abused Child Suffers

This is a good question to which I often have to respond. To know more you can read my articles on my Web site, especially the one about the role of a helping witness in childhood. Unfortunately, the last one, about the cause of our suffering, is now only available in German and French, but will soon be translated. Also, the book *For Your Own Good* is now available free online at www.nospank .net. I am glad that you are fascinated by the story of Hitler; I was also (and still am) fascinated. For a long time I could not understand why only a few understood its importance and import. Now, I understand more: it is because most people (about 95 percent of the world population) were beaten as children. They had to learn very early to suppress their feelings and as adults don't want to be reminded of their suffering. For that reason almost everybody still says today that hitting children is both harmless and necessary.

29 ⌇ Hitler and Murderous Rage

You are right: if a person can, thanks to the help of witnesses, to books, and to the work on his emotions he has done, *acknowledge* the cruelty and stupidity of his parents, he will not become like them. All the monsters known to me, without any exceptions— dictators, Hitler helpers, serial murderers—have idealized their parents.

APRIL 2006

5 ⌇ "How to Punish Children"?

It is true: nobody wants to talk about corporal punishment, not because they didn't experience it, but because they don't want to be reminded of their pain. You are an exception because you want to remember and to talk about this issue. In France there is a magazine called *Psychologies*, and they recently published an article called "How to Punish Children" in which psychologists were asked how to punish. No one said that children shouldn't be punished at all because by punishing them they only learn violence; no, they said that you must punish the child under two years old, otherwise punishment would never be effective. I am afraid we are moving in the old direction of poisonous pedagogy.

6 ❧ Yes, Life Did Owe Them a Living

Why shouldn't your children feel that life owes them a living? Because you were forbidden to feel that life owed you love, acceptance, and joy? But it did owe you all this. You had an extremely cruel childhood, and you are lucky that you didn't abuse your children. But in therapy you should be able to find the suffering of the small, unwanted little girl who knew from the beginning that her existence was hated and couldn't afford to feel the pain consciously. Now you are able to feel it and thus give your children your love. Maybe the book *For Your Own Good* (now available online), and also my last article can help you to understand what I mean.

7 ❧ The Freedom to Feel

At the end of your letter you are almost answering the letter yourself: as adults we must be able to give ourselves the freedom to feel, but if our parents and other caregivers didn't give us this freedom in childhood, we think that we need the permission to be given to us from the outside. Nobody will do this "job" for us, though it is true that some people may make you feel more or less free. Unfortunately, our tendency to repeat old traumas sometimes means that we create a big attachment to people who remind us of our parents. For that reason, we may stay for twenty or thirty years in a marriage where we feel treated like we once were by our mothers and don't dare to express our actual feelings because we are waiting for permission. We must learn that as adults we are the *only* ones responsible for our well-being and authenticity.

13 ↝ Disappointed

I understand and share your disappointment about the lack of interest in the role of our childhood in our lives, but I can't do more than I do: understand and educate others about the reasons for this deplorable indifference. I have written about this issue in all my articles.

15 ↝ Corporal Punishment

When people hear you talking about "child abuse," they can stay at a distance and remain at ease. They do not feel that they have been abused (of course not!), so they think that you are talking about "others," not about them. However, when you raise the topic of corporal punishment, they can't avoid remembering that they were indeed punished (even if they call it harmless spanking), all of them, and that it was painful. But they prefer to avoid the memories of being beaten and so will hardly join you in your endeavor to make this topic known. They avoid the pain.

21 ↝ They Deserve to Be Punished?

You describe in few words the crucial confusion from which *all* mistreated children suffer: they are not allowed to see how cruelly they were treated and have to believe that all the cruelty they endured was because they were bad, because they deserved to be punished. So they feel guilty their entire adult lives. You may be interested in reading my article about feelings of guilt and my last book, *The Body Never Lies*, as well as the book *Breaking*

Down the Wall of Silence. I wish you much understanding from
your therapist.

23 ⌖ *Homosexuals Are Not an Exception*

Why do people expect and demand more from homosexuals than
from heterosexuals? Why do the latter have more of a right to
live unconsciously (with the image of their happy childhood and
a wonderful mother intact) than the former ones? Homosexuals
do even less harm to society because they don't produce children
to exploit them, abuse them, and teach them violence. Of course,
they *can* abuse children and do much harm when they force them
to keep silent. But many heterosexuals do the same, even if they
are parents. So what is the matter with our demands? Do we question why millions of religious people say that beating children is
right because of Solomon's wisdom? No, we don't do anything and
see this as normal. Do we ask why millions of women let their
daughters become sexually mutilated? No, we think that their
religion demands that. But even the Koran does not demand this
at all. It *may* be (I don't know for sure) that the repressed rage of
some men who were beaten as children by their mothers or sisters
unconsciously causes these men to take revenge when they are
adults for what they had to endure in childhood. They honor their
mothers and punish their daughters instead. So they feel good with
this tradition and support it with their whole might. But be careful
and don't give such information to anybody who does not ask you
for it. They would kill you rather than accept the truth that they
suffered abuse in childhood. You know how much time it takes to
confront one's own childhood. So don't try to be a healer by telling

people what they definitely don't want to know. You can only heal yourself, and this is still a great achievement.

26 ❧ Harmful Nonphysical Abuse

Yes, nonphysical abuse can be as harmful as beatings. But it is often less visible. The reason I write mostly about physical abuse is because I want to show that even in the most obvious cases of abuse the adult children tend to deny it. So much more if the abuse was hidden.

MAY 2006

1 ❧ Our Body Does Not Accept Compromise

No, our body doesn't accept the compromise you suggest because it doesn't understand the Bible, or the moral principles of our education. It only understands the language of emotions directed toward *real* parents. To understand my response you should read my book *The Body Never Lies* and the articles on my Web site. To me, forgiveness is even harmful because it conceals the true feelings.

3 ❧ Paralyzed

I was reading your letter and looking for your rage. I didn't find it. But I don't doubt that it is in your body and makes you suffer without end. Hopefully, you will soon decide to *feel* the abuse and the cruelty you suffered from your father and your uncle.

7 ⌖ *Take Seriously What You Already Know*

It seems that you benefited from reading and that you now understand much more about yourself than before. But you need to take seriously what you already know and to stop ignoring your knowledge in the way your mother did. She maintains that she doesn't remember anything, but your body remembers very well. If you are ready to see that it *was* your father in your dream (who else?), you will no longer be compelled to choose cold men and countries where nobody can understand you. I wish you good luck in finding a country where you *want* to be and *can* be understood.

7 ⌖ *Oedipus Complex*

In my opinion the Oedipus complex was one of the ways Freud chose to avoid confronting the whole tragic truth of child mistreatment. On my Web site (see "Articles") you will find an excellent essay by Thomas Gruner on this topic. If you can read more, you can find my own position with many details in my book *Thou Shalt Not Be Aware*. You are also right when you suppose that I understand drug addiction in a much wider context than "the mother's breast." You can read about this in my last book, *The Body Never Lies*, especially the chapter on drugs.

13 ⌖ *Buried Memories and Emotions*

Your letter may indeed help other readers to understand that the memories of our body show us how our parents actually behaved toward us in our first years of life. Your mother may now seem very different to you, and the older she becomes, the more she feels dependent on your care, like a child. But your feelings tell you the true story of the child whose emotions you feel *now*: "I have grown up with the feeling that I am the bad, moody, ungrateful daughter—never able to live up to her standards of niceness and calmness and not able to match her love for me. Consequently, I have felt guilt and a huge sense of obligation to her all of my life." There must be good reasons for feelings like that. Unless you find them, you don't know yourself because you don't know the suffering of the small girl you once were. Before you choose a therapist, try to ask them the questions I suggest to ask on my FAQ list. I wish you much luck in finding the right person.

14 ⌇ *The Body Will Never Understand*

You can *now* understand why your father treated you badly, but this will not help you because your body (the child) will never understand that. It insists on being understood through your acknowledgment of the suffering of the little boy.

15 ⌇ *Depression*

Yes, you are right. I must only add that if you already know your history, without minimizing the suffering of the little boy you were, the depressive phases with time will become less and less frequent, since their role is only one of signalization; they want to make you aware of the fact that very intense, strongly suppressed emotions need to come up and be felt. If this is done, the depressive state disappears immediately. Everybody can have this happen. However, it is impossible to do this work if your body is misguided by antidepressants. It is a shame that so many people don't have this important information, because once they are using this medication, they are unable to have healthy and enlightening experiences.

15 ⌇ *Writing Specifically on Depression*

I have already written about depression (see "Articles" on my Web site and my first book, *The Drama of the Gifted Child*). I agree with many of the things you have written, except your argument that we need years to come out of depression and your assumption that depression is a feeling. It is not; it is a protection against feeling the most authentic emotions, like rage, sadness, fear. Once you can feel them, you are no longer depressed; you gain access to your history, to the suffering of your childhood that is generally painful. So depression is the body's attempt to remind us that we need to do important work in our interest. You are right that the pharmacy and many doctors who offer antidepressants suggest the opposite path: to forget and to deny one's own history. The U.S. soldiers in Iraq use prescribed high doses of antidepressants, yet many have killed themselves.

17 ⌇ *Wishing to Train in Psychotherapy with Children*

Unfortunately, I don't know of any training that would offer what you are looking for. Try to find the suffering of the small girl you were, to become familiar with her and learn to have empathy for her, in the presence of an enlightened witness. This will teach you more than lectures at universities. There is not one university in the world where the effects of child mistreatment are being discussed. Before you decide who should be your therapist, you may want to read my FAQ list.

19 — *C. G. Jung*

I wrote several times about Jung in my books (*Thou Shalt Not Be Aware* and *Banished Knowledge*). Many of his theories, especially the one on archetypes, I regard as a way of escaping from the reality of his childhood, from the trauma of being sexually abused by his father. I wrote among other things that it is easier to fear the archetype of the mean but abstract goddess Kali than to feel the pain of being exploited by the beloved parent. If you read my FAQ list, maybe you will understand why I insist on questioning the future therapist about what he knows about his own childhood and how he worked on it.

JUNE 2006

5 — *Which Books to Start With?*

To start, I would recommend *The Body Never Lies* and the recent articles on my Web site, especially on depression. You are absolutely right that the depression forces you to look into your cruel childhood, the terrible abandonment and injustice you had to endure from your parents. Fortunately, you have your husband on your side, and if you decide to look for a therapist, it could be helpful to read my FAQ list. I wish you good luck with finding the right, well-informed witness!

19 ❧ *The System of Lies*

It is rather surprising that a woman of your profession has the courage to leave, at least partially, the system of denial and open her eyes to the truth of her childhood after having read a book. There are millions of people in your position who never find the courage to do so, nor to question the lies they have been told early in their lives.

You ask me how you can connect with your father. Why should you? Everybody tells you that you must forgive. But you must not, if you want to heal. You can't fool the body; it doesn't let itself be fooled. And it remembers everything, the butcher's knife, the soup cans from the garbage, the beatings, and so many other cruelties suffered by a small girl from a highly perverse man. Why do you jeopardize your health by thinking of your father's childhood? If a man raped you on the street would you speculate about his childhood or would you become furious? The latter would be a healthy reaction. Why is your father an exception? Because God is on his side? Who told you this? The body didn't read the Bible; it insists on the truth, and the small girl would have also if she had been allowed to see the truth. But nobody was there to tell her: you were treated cruelly and have the right to hate him. Unfortunately, you seem to continue to betray your body, yourself, by killing your authentic feelings. In fact, it is exactly this rage that can now help you to heal.

The method of Marshall Rosenberg is very nice and may be helpful to people who were not severely mistreated in childhood. Those who were, however, must find their pent-up, *legitimate* rage and free themselves from the lies of our moral system. As long as they don't do this, their body will continue to scream for the truth.

22 ✑ The Suppressed Rage

You ask me for an answer, but I don't find any question in your letter. You seem to accept what has been done to you and to pay the price with your terrible illness, without rage or without indignation. But it is exactly this rage that could help you to heal. If you want to know my opinion more exactly, you can read my book *The Body Never Lies* and the articles on my Web site.

24 ✑ The Proof

Thank you for your letter. You write: "Expounding the truth will always bring up hell and high water. The resistance and denial of others (in my experience) is proof that one is on the 'right path.'" Unfortunately, you are right. But people who are on the path to themselves hardly want to go back; they find so many unexpected things there that they would not want to miss again.

25 ✑ The Journey I Travel

It is good to know that there *are* some counselors who dare to liberate themselves from the "conformism, distortion and denial" and feel the pain of their own childhood, instead of confusing their clients again, the way their parents already did, by preaching forgetting and forgiveness as well as other destructive ideas. I wish you all the best on your journey.

26 ᴇ *More Solutions?*

It is not my goal to write books about how you can "mitigate your rage against your children," but rather to encourage you to look for the *reasons* for this rage. And I have already written books of this kind. My impression is that you still protect and admire your mother and the way she brought you up and don't allow yourself to criticize her perfectionism and her fear of making an error. No wonder that these emotions of suppressed rage are now directed against your children. I also think that your creativity was stifled from a very early age and it wants to eventually liberate itself—fortunately. But in order to not do it at the expense of your children, you will have to find the suffering of the small girl dependent on a very strict mother. You don't need new books, which should tell you how to be with your children. You know that *very well.* You need only the permission to be yourself. That means to be authentic, even with your rage against people who deserve it, who are *not* your children.

JULY 2006

1 ᴇ *Traditional Morals Among Professionals*

I am glad that, thanks to this mailbox, you have gained more awareness of the traditional morals in the language of professionals, because to make this clear was my purpose when I decided to open this page. Psychoanalysts now go so far as to admit that some patients were not "loved enough" in childhood. But they are still far away from recognizing that most of us had to survive *torture* when our creativity was stifled so that our parents could finally obtain the obedient child they apparently needed. In their language many therapists avoid being "judgmental," and you can feel in this hesitation the fear of a small child that could be punished for "talking back."

3 ⌖ *Hope Amidst Hopelessness?*

I share the hope that you express in your beautiful language: "may we continue remembering and witnessing every tear shed, and hope that humanity will not drown in denial." Your writing shows that it *is* eventually possible to become more and more the person we are born to become, the person we were meant to be, if we dare to *see* what was done to us and if we clearly refuse to tolerate violation. Even if you can't become the child again, by connecting with her as you do and by condemning her mistreatment without hesitations, excuses, etc., your path toward growth continues to *open.* Then you know: never again will you become a victim of such a terrible betrayal like the one you endured from your parents, since you *dare* to see your parents as they *actually are.* We were not mistreated "for our own good," but only because of our parents' denial, which is pure poison to us and nothing else. With all my best wishes for your path of discovery.

4 ⌖ *It Was a Long Night*

If your body is happy with this outcome, it may be okay to you. However, don't forget the small child who had to accept so much violation. Should you have any problems with your body in the future, don't hesitate to remind yourself to empathize with the small child, totally alone with tremendous pain, who speaks so clearly in your letter with these words: "She had totally violated my poor little jungle camp, leaving her mark on every detail! And the worst thing: I was so afraid of her reactions that I never dared to rip those sheets off again during the night. . . . It was a long night, and I have never forgotten how horrible it was, and I never got any understanding from my friends when I told them the story. They said they wished they had such a loving mother as mine, I was an ungrateful bitch."

5 ⌑ A Common Misquote

Your "quotation" is not complete and thus not correct. You write, "Alice Miller writes in her books that the children who were abused will abuse their own children since they do not know how to be any different." But I have *always* written that this happens *only* if they stay in denial as adults. If they have the courage to know how they suffered as children, they *do* know the difference and will *not* repeat what their parents have done to them. *Only* people who don't know that they suffered cruelty in childhood are prone to repeat what they once endured.

8 ⌑ Loneliness

It is indeed very painful to realize how lonely you were as a child. But as you will see, the more you remember and the more you rebel against all these humiliations and the cruel lack of love, the less alone you will feel. You will start to become your knowing witness, a person who never before existed in your life.

8 ୧ *A Suggestion for Your Next Book?*

Thank you very much for your letter. I know the tragic story of Mozart, but I will not write about him. It is very frustrating to describe tragedies of artists' and writers' childhoods and to receive reactions that show little empathy because apparently there are not many people who can feel. To write about the pain of a genius doesn't fit into most people's mentality. Would you like to write about Mozart's love and suffering? I wish you much luck in your life and work.

11 ୧ *Love and Thanks*

I am glad that my books gave you the support you needed when you realized that you were "living a lie." Such a realization is very painful and you need a witness in the process, of course. But it is also very liberating. You are coming out of a prison that was invisible to you until now.

12 ୧ *Genes*

I don't speak about "unresolved childhood traumas" but about the whole atmosphere of families in which children grow up without being allowed to feel and to express their needs. Without a helping witness, these children often learn not to feel at all in order to please their parents and to survive, as I explained it in my book *The Drama of the Gifted Child*. Later, they may develop different illnesses like obsessive neurosis, anorexia, etc., because their bodies need to make them aware of the fact that emotions are very important to a human being; they make it alive. Grown-ups may then realize (in the fortunate cases) that the reasons that made them fear their strong emotions no longer exist and that as adults they are free to feel them and to enjoy themselves.

12 ⤰ *My Mother Didn't Believe Me*

You write: "My analyst concluded that my greatest heartache was not the abuse from my father but rather the fact that my mother didn't love me." This is indeed the most painful insight. Realizing that you were not loved is very hard. But you should not forget that being sexually abused by a father also shows a lack of love. To see both is very disturbing, of course, and you need time to work on your father's betrayal too. Many sexually abused women avoid confronting this betrayal and want to believe that they got some "love" from their father. I wish you good luck and good friends.

14 ⤰ *Physical Abuse, Politics, and Religion*

I agree with you. The consciously *felt* feelings are not dangerous and make us free for finding constructive solutions. But the *denied*, suppressed rage and fear (of parents), covered up by ideologies and religious fanaticism, lead to irrational actions against substitutes that are destructive for both the victim and the aggressor.

19 ⤰ *An Article*

You write: "I somehow doubt I'm alone in saying this, but your books have helped me to understand, feel, and work through so much of my past. It's an ongoing journey, of course, and some days I feel like I have barely set out, but at least it is a journey and, in many ways, a wonderful one." Why is this not enough, to want to write an article and share your experience with others?

19 ⌖ *Childhood Insight and Medication*

You can continue to ask numerous psychiatrists for help, but I doubt whether any of them will speak with you about your childhood. If you want to know what I think about antidepressants, you can find my answer in my last article on my Web site. I understand that you want to "recover quickly," just as perhaps your parents wanted you to stop screaming immediately and not disturb their peace. But healing takes time and requires your compassion for the child you once were. Don't treat yourself like your parents did. Medication can disguise your memories; it can help you to feel better for a while, but the never-acknowledged suffering of the little boy will continue to speak through depression until you are willing to hear what the body (the child) has to tell you.

22 ⌖ *How Do We Change the World?*

We can't change the world; we can only write what we have understood, as you have. Your examples are very telling, and I hope that people who are searching like you will benefit from them.

23 ⌖ *A Question About Violence*

I completely agree with you. Using violent means against dictators and other dangerous people is necessary. Unfortunately, we observe it rather rarely because most people fear these people like they unconsciously fear their parents. For that reason, almost all

Germans applauded Hitler. Having been battered as children, they directed the resulting rage and hatred toward innocent victims in concentration camps and toward their own children. Also, dangerous dictators are viewed with great respect because nobody seems to dare to fully acknowledge what they are doing.

24 ᴇ *Limit-Setting*

You are right; the process of setting limits is a kind of power game that only the adult can win. You know perhaps this kind of limit-setting: A father spanks his son and says: "You pushed your little brother, and he is crying now. I must spank you so that you can learn not to bully someone smaller and weaker than yourself." Is this father aware of the fact that he is doing exactly what he actually wants to forbid (for good reasons)? Probably not. Why? Is he stupid? No, he might even be a professor of psychology, but his first teacher in behavior was his mother, whose lessons he never dared to question. So he does the same to his son. Will we ever change anything as long as once-beaten children (and almost everybody was beaten) are so afraid of their parents that they don't dare to question them? They seem to live in constant fear of the next punishment if they dare to condemn the mistreatment they suffered in childhood. However, only then can they become adult and stop behaving unconsciously like a child scared to death.

24 ᴇ *Grieving Following Therapy*

You write: "I do not have any misgivings about my therapist [why not?], and feel that he was suitably qualified and experienced in his field, but I am left with a level of uncontrollable grief and sense of profound loss." This doesn't sound like a successful end to therapy. Why don't you tell him how you feel? If he no longer wants to listen to you, why don't you look for another therapist? You obviously need help and should take your suffering seriously.

27 ❦ Learning Empathy for Yourself

If you can learn to feel your suppressed but strong emotions in therapy, if you can learn there to empathize with the small child you once were, you certainly will find many answers to the question you ask me. How should I know anything about your life if you don't talk about it?

28 ❦ Poisonous Education

Your story is appalling. How have you survived all these cruelties and perversions? And why do you "want to stay silent"? Don't you feel any need to rebel and to scream loudly about what has been done to you?

28 ❦ Never Too Late

I read your letter and am very sorry that I can't respond to it, because I feel that whatever I would write, it will not reach you as long as you take antidepressants. The one thing I can tell you without hesitation is that, in my experience with myself and others, it is *never* too late to feel and understand our truth, namely the suffering of the small child we once were. This means to feel for the first time his suppressed fear and rage, which would liberate your energies and the joy of life. But, unfortunately, the medication makes all this impossible.

30 ⌘ Marlon Brando

I haven't read the book by Marlon Brando, but I can guess what I would find there. We don't have lists of therapists; I can only suggest that you read my FAQ list when you are looking for a therapist. Also, reading *The Body Never Lies* may be helpful. For many years now I have been asking the publisher and the author of *Reclaiming Your Life* to remove my preface from the book because I no longer recommend it. Unfortunately, I have never received any answer and my request has simply been ignored. Obviously—as you now let me know—my text is still being used against my will because it may be not in the interest of the publisher to do what I asked for.

30 ⌘ Using the AM Paintings as a Tool

At first I was surprised by your mention of the Rorschach test that has been used since the 1950s for diagnostic aims, which I don't appreciate at all. But then, after a short time, I found your idea very convincing and I like it. Of course, not every psychologist could work with this "tool," but for sensitive people like you, regarding these paintings together can enable a real emotional contact with the suffering person. If you ask what they feel or see when they regard a painting, they may come in touch with their own feelings in a much deeper way than if they only talk about their childhoods and are blocked by fears of their parents. If you have already had some experiences of this kind, please let us know.

AUGUST 2006

2 ⦿ *Honor Thy Father and Mother*

If your metaphysical and metaphorical understanding of the Bible helps you to heal, there is nothing to say against it. But if you were not a mistreated child, you were not wounded, so I don't understand what you need to heal from. On the other hand, if you were beaten and humiliated, don't forget to also honor the small child who survived inside of you, whose suffering was never acknowledged, who can't understand the Bible nor your interpretations of it, and who is still hoping in pain that you eventually may *honor his suffering* and take it seriously.

6 ⦿ *I Cry Without Reason*

You say that you "cry without reason." Apparently you refuse to know the actual reasons of your plight and you try "to conceal the truth." Nobody cries without reason. Read the book *The Body Never Lies* to find more answers to your questions.

6 ⦿ *Response to a Letter on Limit-Setting*

I completely agree with what you are saying here and am very grateful for your references to the helpful Web sites. I haven't yet checked them, but I trust your judgment because I know you and your history. To me you are living proof that even the most abused victim is not condemned to repeat the endured abuse on her children thanks to her growing *consciousness*. Actually, children could be our best teachers when we carefully observe their (always positive) reaction to our respectful attitude.

9 ❧ With Thanks . . .

You write: "I still feel pity for them [your parents] and don't wish their pain to be any worse as I guess they have lived with it longer than I." I can understand your concerns but feel at the same time that here might be the blockade that hinders you from having pity for the battered boy you were and for his strong feelings of being discouraged from life. He could not share his pain with anybody after the death of his grandmother. To understand what I have in mind, please read my article on the reasons for our suffering and the one about feelings of guilt (both in the section "Articles" on my Web site). You also write: "I realized that they will *probably* never change their ways and I was wasting my time and energy." Why should they change? The word "probably" shows that the hope of the small child is still very present in your mind. Parents that could beat their small children without pity usually don't change.

16 ❧ My Painting

My experience was that I had no special programs or intention. I just enjoyed playing with colors and the liberty of doing what I wanted, and what came out was my childhood, my suffering of being alone and never understood. I don't know of other painters who would tell me the same story.

18 ᴈ *Expectations*

You write in your letter that now you take full responsibility for your actions toward your son, and you add, "I therefore expect my own parents to do the same: nothing more, nothing less." I think that as long as you still expect this—or anything else—from your parents, you are not free from them. But one day you will become free because you want to and you understand very much already. I wish you the insight you need to no longer wait for your parents to change.

22 ᴈ *Blocked Memories*

You are right; your memories are blocked by fear. Have you read any of my books? I would recommend *The Drama of the Gifted Child* and *For Your Own Good*. And if you start to feel anything about your childhood, write again. By the way, your feeling that you were never together with your parents in the same room shows already how terribly alone and abandoned you must have been in your childhood. Good memories are usually not blocked. It seems that there was nothing good you could remember.

30 ᴈ *Looking for a Therapist*

I am very sorry that I can't recommend a therapist to you. For that reason, I wrote the FAQ list so that you can check if the therapist you are talking to will be on your side and will not try to give you "lessons" in the traditional way. You should also read my last book, *The Body Never Lies*, and the articles on my Web site to be better informed before you choose a therapist. I wish you good luck!

31 ⚭ *Positive Anger*

You write: "I want to do whatever it takes to drive my point home, and you cannot do that with a weak heart." You are right; anger is often our protector from blindness, cowardice, cooperating with cruelty. Your illness is a language. Can it be that it wants to make you aware that your anger toward your parents is justified and should not be withheld?

SEPTEMBER 2006

7 ⚭ *Chronic Muscular Pains*

I am sorry that I can't help you. It is a very painful illness and I don't doubt that it is connected to traumatic experiences in childhood. But patients with these symptoms usually don't want to discover what happened to them in their childhood and to feel the helplessness that they endured.

8 ⚭ *Benign Abuse?*

You write: "So many 'puzzle' pieces continue to fall into place for me." I am glad for you. And if you are in trouble again, try to look closer at the "benign" abuse you suffered and try to imagine how you felt as a baby with bound arms to prevent your scratching of the eczema on your face. And you may then ask yourself why you suffered from eczema so young. There are so many kinds of torture for a small kid that we adults consider to be benign.

16 ⪼ A Dream of the Gifted Child

I was very moved by your wonderful dream and your very telling letter. I do feel that your dream can be explained rationally and I hope that you will be able to do so as soon as you stop idealizing your childhood. Of course, this is a process that might take much time, but the dream will stay with you as your knowing witness, and will reorient you each time you try to fool yourself—because the pain may sometimes seem unbearable. It is rarely so. Usually, feeling the pain and ceasing attempts to understand and pity the parents brings a great deal of relief and insight.

21 ⪼ Emotional Neglect

I think that neglect (emotional abuse) is as painful as physical abuse, sometimes even more so, but both are denied. I emphasize the physical abuse to show how even people who do recall the slaps and severe beatings they received from their parents believe as adults that they have been loved. It happens even more if there were no beatings at all (which is very rare). Your body may remind you now of what you don't want (*yet*) to recall.

OCTOBER 2006

1 ⪼ The Truth Will Set You Free

You write: "Since beginning to talk about these buried experiences and feelings, I find myself with more energy and have been able to work part-time consistently for almost two years . . . such a liberating feeling . . . after nearly a decade of chronic fatigue syndrome."

The fatigue syndrome appears if you try to suppress what you absolutely need to say because you are afraid of being punished if you try to speak out. However, the energies will come back; you will feel that it is worthwhile to live once you can live with your own truth. I hope that my other books, especially *The Body Never Lies*, will encourage you to fight against the scandalous practice of the "treatment" centers. Fighting against the lies can give you back the energy you have lost while staying silent. I wish you the courage you need to try again and again.

7   The Drama . . .

Thank you for your letter. I think that you will succeed to liberate yourself from the prison of your past because you want to know exactly what happened in your childhood and you have the good fortune of sisters who want to know as well. I recommend that you read my last book, *The Body Never Lies*, and the articles on my Web site.

9   Youth Gangs—"Maras"— in Central America

I am willing to answer all questions concerning the causes of violence, but I don't know of any government that would be interested in my answers, because almost all of us were beaten as children. Thus most of us are afraid of punishment if we realize the truth. Instead of confronting it, we deny the suffering of our past and are unable to understand the rage of the youth. We speculate a lot about the causes of violence, while carefully avoiding the issue of child mistreatment, and thus are helpless in the face of the destructive behavior of gangs. However, it is more than under-standable that children who learn from their parents' violence in their first years of life will keep these lessons in the structure of their brain, mostly forever—if society continues to stay blind.

12 ℮ *Forgiveness Was a Farce*

Isn't it amazing to discover one's own denial? And the freedom this discovery brings us? With this experience your path is open. It takes time to walk on it, but you can't be fooled again.

16 ℮ *What Is Corporal Punishment?*

To me, corporal punishment means injuring, attacking, offending, and beating the body of another person and pretending that this act of aggression is "for his own good." It is then called spanking, educating, etc. This kind of violence toward children contains a lie because a child doesn't learn anything good in a state of fear; it only teaches the child to use violence in adulthood. Beating or spanking a child also contains a big danger, because the brain of a small child is use-dependent; its experience later becomes its structure, and to regard violence as good and normal becomes ingrained. To me, so-called corporal punishment is nothing else than disguised *child abuse*. More information can be found at the rich and interesting Web site www.nospank.net, where its director, Jordan Riak, provides a lot of online material and a very informative booklet.

18 ⊱ *Journal for Miller Studies*

As you see, there are not many who are not afraid of invoking punishment if they acknowledge the role of parents in producing violence and psychosis. Since almost all of us were beaten as children, the fear of punishment is still with us unless we work on it. Do you know people who would have the courage to write for such a journal?

19 ⊱ *How to Believe I'm Basically "Good" When I've Made My Son Feel "Bad"*

You can't change the past. If you can't see yourself as a good person, maybe you can see yourself as an honest person who wants to realize her truth without fooling herself. It would mean acknowledging that your parents didn't provide you with patterns of love for a child. They did the opposite. Now you have a choice, and your son will feel it as soon as you stop blaming yourself for what your parents did.

20 ⊱ *To Find the Poison Is Healing*

You say that your patients leave your treatment happy because they found out what poisoned their whole life. It is exactly what therapists need to understand. But most of them are afraid of seeing and feeling how their parents treated them and so offer their patients morality instead of empathy. Yes, you are right: therapy gives us the courage to find the poison in our lives and to get rid of it by learning to have empathy for the mistreated child we once were.

20 ஃ Letter from Poland

Your incredible letter is proof that you can recover if you want to know your truth, if you can overcome your fear of it. And it shows that it is easier to succeed without a therapist than with one who is himself afraid of his truth.

21 ஃ Age and Change

I am not surprised that you can change even after seventy, because it is not age that makes us change, but the willingness to know our own history and the courage to recognize the things that poisoned our lives.

24 ஃ I Am Becoming

Thank you for your letter and your trust. Your life was for a long time shaped by the logical consequences of your childhood—as is always the case. But you find the courage to confront your history and have the good fortune to do it with an enlightened witness. Even if there is much suffering on this path, you are no longer in danger because you *know* now what happened, and you *want* to know. I wish you all my best and hope that my books and my paintings (on my Web site) will help you to bear your truth and to *believe* in what your art is telling you.

26 ஃ Freedom

Indeed, the true life begins when you stop trying to please others and start to take care of yourself.

26 ᘒ Thank You So Much

I was moved by your letter, and I am glad that my books will give company and compassion to the sad and lonely child you have discovered and are going to protect and love.

29 ᘒ Help Please

You write: "It's like there's a volcano of rage inside that I am trying to control so that someone will be sympathetic and want to help me." It is precisely this fully legitimate rage that can help you if you express and understand it. The depression and panic attacks come when you try to control your rage and other feelings. Since *The Drama* helped you so much, why don't you read the other books, especially *The Body Never Lies*? You need a therapist who can help you feel the plight of the small, abused, rejected, and neglected child you once were. On my Web site, under "Articles," you will find the FAQ list that can help you find a therapist who is not afraid to see how parents destroy the lives of their children. If you think you should sacrifice your life for your parents because they are old, take the photo of yourself with the bottle and ask yourself: Whom could I have asked then to give me a warm breast? My mother is here, looking at me, and has no pity. She didn't teach me to care about me. However, I will learn to do it. I will learn from my body, from my *feelings*—even from my justified rage—to love *me*.

30 ᘒ Also in Japan

Thank you for testifying that what I describe in my books is not limited to the Christian culture. I don't doubt that the same mentality governs the whole world: you are allowed to abuse your child and call it education, but you are forbidden to see the crimes of your parents. Everybody is afraid of being beaten again if they see and name these crimes. However, as long as you don't dare to see them, you are compelled to repeat them with your children. For that reason, we must learn to *know* what we are doing and why.

30 ⌒ *Who Will Want Me?*

You write: "It has taken forty years to realize what my mother has done to me, and now it seems I am stuck there and selfishly cannot deal with anything else." It is normal that, having recently realized the early rejection of your mother, you now need time—much time. And please don't call it selfish if you eventually decide to have compassion for the rejected child you were then. Don't take any medication, for it will hinder you in understanding your feelings, the deep sorrow, the rage and other strong emotions that have been stored up in your body for forty years! Let them come to the surface and try to express them in your therapy. You will see that talking about how you feel will help you more than taking pills. You *can* survive a night without sleeping; the next night you may sleep. Let the dreams come up. Don't fear them. They are your friends because they will inform you about the plight of the small girl rejected by her mother. And don't think that nobody will want you if your mother didn't. There are other people in the world who are not like your mother and who may love you once you no longer deny what has happened to you.

NOVEMBER 2006

12 ⌇ Discovering the Anger and Sharing It

Isn't it wonderful that you were able to meet yourself, the real you, the angry child that has waited for so long to be heard and understood? Now your adult self has come into the prison of this child and said: "You are safe, you can talk to me, you have plenty of reasons to be enraged, I will listen to them and protect you so that nothing like that can happen to you again. You have survived a hell and you need to tell me how you feel, the words are coming now, what a relief! If you stay silent, these feelings of hate may poison you, but not when you are talking and sharing them with me." I congratulate you on your success. It is certainly painful to see the truth and to feel the hatred, but it is not dangerous; it is liberating. You will see it soon.

12 ⌇ Questioning the Family

You write: "In the traditional family the children belong to their parents, who have legal power over them. The children are isolated from the rest of society; they have to respect their parents, regardless of what the parents actually do; they have to obey their parents and to be loyal toward them. And the parents, often with the help of the state, can do almost anything to subdue their children; they can use the whole range of physical and mental tortures against their children." You certainly are right, but why shouldn't we be able to change the patterns of the family instead of rejecting family altogether? And what do you suggest instead of the familial institution? A child needs a mother and a father, but of course they don't need the hypocrisy, the abuse, the exploitation, and the terror. We must work on enlightening parents so that families become the place of safety, truth, love, and honest communication. We can't do this by writing nice words, but by informing parents that they disguise the brutality they endured as children by denying it and repeating it carelessly in their own family dynamic. In this way they protect their parents and produce violent people again and again. I agree with you that families based on the now-existing system are the source of violence in our society, and I do what I can to make this visible.

13 &c Freedom and Mourning

It is normal that freedom can't stay forever and that we will have moments when we may be reminded of our past; but we will be better equipped to deal with the old memories as soon as we know the pain of our childhood. Once you have learned to care for your child, you will be able to let her feel the old fears and at the same time to protect her and find the solution to conflicts in the present. Then freedom will come back. But you will never again want to live without your history, and so memories will still have access to your mind—if they need to find this access. As you show, you could not prevent the therapy group and the therapist from wanting to abuse you, but you were strong enough to realize what happened and to leave. The child in yourself had the freedom to feel, and the adult you have now become protected the child by taking action.

14 ❧ My Father Did Nothing to Save Me

You wrote that you wanted to read my other books; I wonder what you will write us after that? Your father might have enabled you to see how your mother has treated you and this is absolutely important for your later life. Most children can't even see the injustice. But your father didn't save you from the maltreatment and he scared you terribly with his violence. I wish you the courage to see how you suffered from him. Maybe the articles on my Web site can help.

17 ❧ The Helpless Helpers

I think that even new methods that already acknowledge the many traumas endured in childhood are still unable to help if they don't encourage the clients to clearly see that they were not only submitted to some traumas but lived for many, many years as helpless children in a climate of an unbearable terror without "knowing witnesses." Only if we as therapists can bear this knowledge can we help the survivors of these crimes to *rebel* against them, to stop protecting their parents from their rage and to liberate themselves from the feelings of guilt; they pay for this with countless illnesses. If you read my article on indignation and other articles on my Web site, you will understand why my books are not known in Florida or elsewhere. Who wants to know what Dad or Mom have really done? The therapists don't want to know it either. So many of them prevent their clients from acknowledging the truth. They don't want to be bothered with my books because these books confront them with their history. There are not many seeking this confrontation, as you obviously are. Most prefer to stay the "help-ers," without knowing their history. But this actually doesn't work. The body rebels at the end.

17 ᴇ A Case in Mexico

You write: "Your books should be given to us in the hospitals when we take our babies home. But I understand how threatening to some people they might seem. Especially because we don't know what to do then; I mean if we don't use physical force, how can we "control" kids? In Mexico, this is a very important issue; we feel we must have control over the defenseless." Why should we have control over the defenseless? Only because we learned to do so from our parents. And religion agrees with this. If we dare to see the crimes that come from this control, we no longer feel helpless and we see that we *can* change much, very much: we can change this mentality and leave the patterns of our parents behind.

21 ᴇ Remembering

I agree with you. *All of them*, all of *us*. But there are, however, some who want to know, and this makes the big difference. I hope that the more people want to know, the easier it will be to break down the wall of silence and lies. But maybe this will take centuries, because the millions of children who are being beaten today will grow up as "beaters" and go on to preach "discipline" tomorrow, without a visible end.

26 ~ Speaking the Truth

I think that you told her the truth, and this is always better than feeding her with illusions and lies, because it will give her the strength to later acknowledge her own truth and to bear it.

28 ~ Using the Rage to Understand

You write: "Sometimes I don't speak up to people who've hurt me because I'm overwhelmed by rage and anxiety that I know don't belong in the present situation." But you say that they hurt you, and this is real. Why don't you speak up? The rage is a source of information. If you don't use this information and continue to avoid understanding it, you will accumulate more and more rage in your life. Try to understand what makes you angry in the present.

DECEMBER 2006

1 ~ Why I Remain Silent

So you found the reason why you don't react to being treated badly; you are *afraid* of then being assaulted even more. But why do you feel ashamed? You are not guilty, it is them; *they* should be ashamed of treating you so badly. However, you write: "I feel surprise, shame, and anger when she does this, and no words come out of my mouth. Of course, it's my problem that I feel shame. This was how I felt when I was a child and my parents criticized me (which was constantly)—ashamed. If I said something to defend myself, they would have one or a combination of these reactions:

screaming more criticisms at me, contemptuous comments, physical violence or the threat of it. Afterward, I would be shunned, hardly spoken to, and looked at with disgusted eyes. I eventually stopped trying to speak up for myself." This was what you did as a child in danger. But now you are not a child and not in danger. You can use words to express your feeling of anger. If somebody becomes angry at you because you were honest, it is *their* anger, not yours, and it is up to them to deal with their feelings. If you go on to suppress your feelings to spare others your truth, your true reactions, you will accumulate anger, as I wrote before, and you risk eventually becoming ill. I wish you the courage you need to take your feelings seriously and stay honest.

1 ⟠ The Fiercest Taboo

I am very sorry that your very important letter was lost and thank you for having sent it again. It is deeply moving and shows what probably millions of children have to suffer but never are able to put into words. You write: "She told me hundreds of times, maybe thousands of times, not to make a mountain out of a molehill. I learned to make every drastic horror into a very small black dot that I could swallow and hide from everyone. I learned to make tiny molehills out of mountains." Yes, so many do the same, and they pay for it with severe illnesses and blindness, which make them hypocritical mothers too. It is so terrible that your mother wanted you to love the monster of your father, who mistreated you sexually and physically over many years, because "who else would love him?" This is more than simple hypocrisy; it is a multiple crime because it kills the true emotions of a child and brings to her brain a confusion that could last her whole life. Fortunately, you escaped this fate; you seem to see clearly now what your mother has done. This will save your life, I think.

3 ⧉ A Question

You write: "Around this time my father started behaving aggressively. For no apparent reason he would become extremely angry with me, jerk me away from what I was doing, take me home, lock me in my room after a severe spanking (buttocks and legs), and then leave me there." Then you write: "Am I wanting the impossible? My abuse was not like the horror you describe in your books or in the letters on your Web site" [AM: I don't agree with you], "is there a possibility that I can be friends with my parents without harming myself?" My answer is *no*. It will be easy for you to understand my answer if you read my book *The Body Never Lies*.

3 ⧉ A Painful Relationship

Why do you need a relationship that makes you suffer, with a man who already tells you that he would like to spank his children in the future? Does he remind you of anybody you knew in your childhood?

5 ⧉ Compassion for People Who Hurt Us

Your letter shows how much you have been suffering in your life and that you have certainly seen others suffer too. I think that your profession has provided you with all that one needs to understand how people become criminals. But as you say, there are only a few who are ready to see the truth with which they are daily confronted. You write: "My scars are deep but not without compassion for those who created them." Maybe you will suffer less when you give up compassion for those who created your deep scars. You can at least try and see what will happen. And you can tell us then how you feel. Having compassion for people who hurt you hurts your body and soul. Be true to yourself. You certainly need unconditional love and compassion—for the small boy who suffered so much without being guilty—but not for the perpetrators. With the moral lessons we received as children, it is hard to become emotionally honest, but it is possible if you dare to know your story. And you seem to dare.

8 ℮ Feeling Overwhelmed

Many psychologists think that *The Drama* is "all they need." They seem to be frightened by my most recent books, which show the histories of mistreatments, the cruelty of parents, and the effects of denial. I wish you the courage you need to discover the truth of your childhood. Whatever you choose to do, don't take antidepressants. They will only hinder you in finding the cause of your depression.

8 ℮ Teaching to Hate

You write: "My opinion is that corporal punishment teaches us to hate. Not to be better persons." You are absolutely right, as in most statements that you made. Why do you call yourself stupid? Obviously, your family is stupid and you refuse to see this; you prefer not to acknowledge it. But it is you who will have to pay the price for this lie. Do you want to pay it?

13 ֍ *Media Request—Child Sexual Abuse*

I agree with what you have written and can confirm that your reference to my work is correct. The statistics you quote (40 to 80 percent) may be based on reports of perpetrators who *deny* that they have been victims. If they were aware of their histories, of the suffering they had to endure in their childhood, they would have been empathic with themselves and also respectful of other children. They would be unable to molest them. It is precisely this denial of their suffering that drives them to abuse others. And the same denial drives the media to use so-called scientific statistics in order to disguise the truth.

14 ֍ *A Personal Question*

Be patient with yourself. It seems that you are on the right path because you *want* to discover the truth. But doubts are normal. Who wants to believe that what is incredible was indeed real? And was done to a small helpless human being? It takes time to admit the truth, and you need the company of a therapist who will not preach to you about forgiveness.

16 ֍ *Personal Comment and Question*

You write: "I'm still in therapy, I have changed so much in just four months, and I love logic." I am positive that you will find the answer you ask me for on your own because *you love logic*.

16 ❧ Where Can I Share Ideas?

Nobody is stopping you from sending *The Drama* to Spielberg or to other filmmakers, but I guess that it is easier to make films for millions of dollars than to look into one's own history. Many great filmmakers succeed in brilliantly showing the tragedy of their own childhoods again and again without being willing to feel it. Instead they make fun of it and earn much admiration because this is what most people wish they could do.

16 ❧ From Beijing Again

It seems that you found the right therapist and so you can feel the rage about what happened to the small girl. If you can feel indignation toward your parents and uncle without wanting to protect them, you are on your way to protecting the child in you who once suffered so much without any witnesses. This process takes time: be patient and don't expect miracles from yourself.

20 ❧ The Forgotten Rape

I never heard about any perverse sexual fantasies that were not the effects of sexual abuse endured in childhood. In most cases, these causes are denied or disguised, but fortunately you seem to see them clearly. Once you can acknowledge the rage against your parents for the crimes you already know, you will not need the fantasies that scare you so much. In having them, you protect your parents from your rage and yourself from the truth. But your parents no longer have power over you unless you give it to them. If not, you can feel your rage and liberate yourself.

21 ⌖ Illusions Disguised as Spirituality

Your reply is revealing to me because in my opinion the word "spirituality" in most cases covers something that is not clear. In your concept I don't see the path to growth but rather the repetition and continuation of the child's dependency on illusions. My experience gave me a very different view into illness and healing. If you have enough time, you can read the letters published here and see that growing and healing begin when former victims of mistreatment start to confront themselves with the cruelty of their upbringing, without illusions about the "love" of a higher power and without blaming themselves for projections. They allow themselves to feel their authentic emotions without moral restrictions and in this way become eventually true to themselves. But the twelve steps continue to keep the ACA [Adult Children of Alcoholics] in the former dependency of the child: fear, self-blame, and permanent overstrain. A person who eventually, painfully realizes that she was never loved, can, based on this truth, learn to love herself and her children. But a person who lives with the illusion that she was indeed loved by a Higher Power, though she has missed feeling this love, will probably blame herself in the old manner for her lack of gratitude and will tend to demand the love from her children. In doing so she will pass on the blame to her children if they don't behave in the way that she wishes, together with the lie that she learned in her so-called recovery.

24 ⌖ Paranoia?

Trust your feelings and your thoughts. Take them seriously. It happens quite often that people who read my books don't feel understood by therapists who are scared by the issue of childhood. You are free to ask questions and to test the received answers. The child was afraid of punishment when she had doubts; the adult has the right to question *everything* without being punished. Your doubts may be very essential, very important messages. Listen to them. They have nothing to do with paranoia.

30 ♁ *Unfathomable!*

I do feel your gratitude and can understand it. How could it happen that you worked for ten years on your "recovery" and nobody has yet helped you to feel the rage toward your mother? Her crime is unfathomable to me. She wanted to "give a lesson to her three-year-old girl" who came bleeding because of being penetrated? I've heard a great deal about cruelties that parents are able to perform, but this case is beyond any limits. And how is it possible that you can only now feel compassion for this betrayed child? Fortunately, you can. I think that a mother without any compassion made your whole childhood a hell. Do you have a good friend who could accompany you if you decide to go to your mother and tell her how you feel about what she did? In any case you need to tell it to *yourself* and to rebel against this enormous madness. I am sure that your symptoms will disappear, because you feel already the empathy for the child you once were and you want to know the whole truth. You will thus certainly succeed.

31 ♁ *Brainwashing in Medical Training I*

I completely agree with you and share your concerns. You write: "There is a lot of the same 'group-think,' authoritarianism, use of humiliation and rank, to not only "whip into shape" new doctors, but also to negate, wipe out, or pathologize true *compassion* in the treatment of the patient. And it is truly amazing the amount of rationalization and denial that occurs with this." And you write further: "I have attempted (without success) to discuss this with other health care professionals, but it seems that everyone has been so completely 'brainwashed' that they see no inherent problems with their education nor with the system itself. I would be interested if anyone had any experience or comments on this." We are publishing your letter here in the hope that other physicians who feel the same discomfort will share some suggestions. Maybe some of them have an idea about how doctors can be encouraged to trust their feelings and take interest in the childhood history of their patients. In my opinion, this could certainly reduce prescriptions of unnecessary and sometimes harmful medication.

III

FROM JANUARY
TO DECEMBER

2007

JANUARY 2007

5 ↭ *Living Your Life*

Fortunately, you now live your life. Isn't it amazing that we feel better as soon as we dare to see how awful we felt before? Unfortunately, most of us expect punishment if we dare to look into our childhood.

6 ↭ *Brainwashing in Medical Training II*

You write: "I have used the lack of compassion I experienced to heighten the compassion I feel for my own patients, with incredibly rewarding results." Have you already tried to ask your patients if they were beaten in childhood? I suggested it many times to many physicians, but they were afraid to do so. Only one of them did it and was surprised that a long story of a chronic illness came to an end after the pains of the childhood had come to the surface. Unfortunately, many doctors keep their own secrets to themselves and thus can hardly offer compassion to their patients; their artificial security may fall away. They don't know that this look at the past could give them and their patients the opportunity to live their own authentic lives, without the lies and without the secrets that protect parents.

9 ↤ *Follow-Up to Your Question*

You write: "I have not asked my patients if they were beaten in childhood, mostly because my patients are still in childhood (I am a pediatric cardiologist, so my patients are children), and parents almost always are with their children at the clinic visit." If I were a pediatrician, I would ask *every* parent whether they spank their children and tell them never to do this. Even and precisely in the presence of the child. I would tell them that a spanked child grows up in fear, pain, and with suppressed rage that for many can only be expressed through illness. Why should a permanently frightened child *not* become ill?

16 ↤ *Need Help*

We don't have any lists of therapists. I hope that my articles will help you to understand the small abandoned and tortured girl you once were that now, fortunately, starts to feel. If you try to understand and to love her, you can help her more than traditional therapists can.

19 ↤ *The Key*

You think it is strange that you felt relieved when the woman told you that you were sexually abused by your father. It is not at all strange. Your denial didn't allow you to feel normal reactions to the abuse: the sorrow and the rage. You couldn't understand their meaning, like you couldn't understand your abnormal rejection of your first newborn. But he gave you the key: by rejecting him, you actually rejected your father. The woman gave you the information that liberates you from doubt. The taboo is not only universal in Poland; it is everywhere, trying to silence the victims. But some of them, like you, begin to realize that they have to pay a high price for that denial, and they refuse to pay it if they want to heal. I wish you the courage that you need to stay with your truth, to stay on the side of the exploited little child you once were—and to save your health.

19 & A Book About Fighting Depression

I am glad that you succeeded in liberating yourself from the depression by having admitted the whole, extremely painful truth of a child with an alcoholic father. It is understandable that you want to become a witness to others who also suffered severe abuse in their childhood. Unfortunately, I can't write you a preface, nor can I read your manuscript. But if you honestly stay with your truth, if you don't preach forgiveness, or tolerance and understanding for endured cruelty, and if you don't offer the flight into a nebulous "spirituality," your readers may feel understood and supported by an enlightened witness whom they can trust.

22 & Confusing

Around 1997, I met two persons who became addicted to primals in the hope of eventually liberating themselves from their past and emptying the "pool of pain." They tried to do their best: they cried and cried, without any resolution. They felt not good enough if they didn't succeed in healing. At the same, time they were unable to question even the cruelest behavior of their parents. To me this was exactly the reason why they were blocked. I think that you don't need to recall every traumatic event if you deeply feel the devastating effect that your mother's or father's hatred for you created in your soul. It is hubris, and it doesn't make much sense to forgive oneself. Of course, flashbacks may come again and again and will help you to understand your feelings (of the past and of today) once you are open to them. You can find my concept of effective therapy in my recent articles on my Web site.

22 ❧ Healing the Trauma

Probably, there was not one trauma but a long history of pain that you don't mention here. But if you dare to *feel* this pain, you can try to resolve the old trauma in the *present* time by responding in another way than that of the agonized child—by defending yourself. You are now an adult and can try without taking the risk of dying. At the same time, the old wounds can heal.

23 ❧ Before We Have Children

I can understand why you question my statement, and I agree with you that it would be better if we could learn to feel and understand the tragedy of our childhood earlier, at least before we have children. But many people of a younger age are still dependent on their parents, financially and emotionally, and they are less motivated to confront them. They may suffer from lies, but they usually hope that everything will be okay once they have their own family, a partner and children. The realization that the illusions don't work— because the repressed and thus unresolved memory of their cruel childhood is still in their body—comes later. Then the time comes when it becomes essential to confront ourselves with our truth: essential for our health, even for our life, if we don't want to fool ourselves by taking antidepressants or choosing beliefs (religious, political, or sectarian) that help to maintain our illusions. This is not a rule, of course (as you see, there are still exceptions), but young people sometimes write here very enraged about the manipulations of their parents. They feel suffocated, but still live with the parents who make them suffer daily and don't dare to move. In most cases, they are too afraid to see the truth and to take their feelings— *themselves*—seriously. As children, they learned to never take their feelings seriously, but rather to say, "It is OK."

25 ⌒ *Why Mental Illness?*

You are right to ask for more explanations, but you will find them in my books and at least in the twenty-one points on my Web site under "Flyers." I can't repeat here what I have written in all my books, and I can't avoid being simplistically labeled as "antipsychiatric" by people who don't take the time to read and understand my work. Concerning your sister, I think that only *she* could say if and how she had to suffer in *her* childhood if she had had a compassionate witness of her pain. As she obviously didn't have anyone, only her body knows her history; her mind can't know it. It does everything it can to disguise it with physical symptoms because the painful truth is unbearable in isolation. However, it is only the truth that can heal. Now your sister has her illness, her medication, and her family who sees the causes of her illness only in her genes. But fortunately she also has a sister who obviously wants to know more.

26 ᴄ *Mental Illness and "Supportive Families"*

You write: "To be able to say about another human being one must have monitored that person every second, 24–7, from the moment of birth, and even more important, one must know for sure how that other person feels and thinks." But we have so many diagnostic labels that help to disguise the abuse. And this is exactly the reason why people MUST become severely ill: they are in total isolation with their pain. Nobody wants to see the facts that explain the "illness."

27 ᴄ *Alzheimer's Disease and Poisonous Pedagogy*

I don't have any doubt that Alzheimer's is a flight response to flash-backs of a painful childhood that come more frequently for older people because their resistance against remembering the truth is weakened by advanced age.

29 ᴄ *Postpartum Depression*

It is absolutely normal that the birth of a child, above all of the first one, triggers in the young mother emotions connected to her own birth. If she gets help, thanks to the presence of a doula, for instance, she can consciously experience these feelings even if they were traumatic and have thus been hidden for a long time. But if she is left alone, with not the slightest understanding from the people around her, she will repress again the emotional "memories" of her own birth and instead of accepting them will get what is called depression. The label "postpartum" suggests that this is a normal reaction to a birth. But the normal reaction to having given space to a new human being is joy, if the mother also was received with joy and not with fear or hatred when she was born.

31 ᘒ Getting Free

You write: "I do not feel unable to cope *as long as I keep away from the lies which surround me*. That is what my body is telling me: that I must escape to be with my damaged child. But there is no language or cultural space which affirms this need. I'll find a way, but I just really needed to share this with you." You are right: there are not many who affirm the need for the truth. But if you dare to carefully look at everybody's story, it is always the *lie* that makes them ill. And the body always rebels.

FEBRUARY 2007
2 ᘒ The Body Never Lies

Some people make the discovery that they were beaten as babies very late in their life, at your age or even later, when they are strong enough to bear this truth. Some never discover it; they take antidepressants instead.

2 ᘒ Abuse of an Entire Generation?

You write: "Horrifying though it is to believe that a generation of parents would rather see their children dead than have their basic social assumptions challenged, I have come to believe that there is an element of truth to this." I am afraid that this important quote not only concerns one generation, but many.

2 ⟐ Unraveling the Abuse

You write: "Why do I still want this man? Why do I still think I love him? Is it my father-hunger? Bulimia, anorexia, alcoholism, self-hatred, have plagued my life for twenty-five years. . . . I'm so exhausted from punishing myself. . . ." So you do know very well the answers to your questions. What you have yet to do is realize how your father treated you, how much you suffered because of *him,* and to rebel against *him.* You write that you loved him so much; why did you? When you get rid of this "love," substitutes will no longer be necessary.

2 ⟐ Your Emotions—Your Friends

You are asking, "Have you heard of other cases like mine?" Your case is not at all an exception. In almost all cases the family (or the institution) protects the abuser and they put the blame on the victim who insists on the truth. So she, or he, feels abandoned and isolated because other victims prefer to stay in denial and refuse to be witnesses. But eventually it is the truth that will set you free; working in a group will enable you to gain compassion and witnesses to your suffering. But above all, your emotions of sorrow and rage will become your best friends; they will protect you from the lies, denial, and becoming ill.

4 ⟐ Forgiveness

I wrote about the damaging function of forgiveness in articles on my Web site and in my books, above all in the books *Banished Knowledge* and *The Body Never Lies.*

5 ❧ In Pain but Conscious

I agree with you when you write, "I cannot but state that those who hurt their children are simply insane." But I must add that they became like this because they were beaten as small children and then learned to believe that this madness was okay. I think that parents who, like you now, can understand how hurtfully they have treated their children can tell them that it was wrong and apologize. In this way, they can help them to become conscious *before* they have children of their own. They may not accept these apologies if they are in denial, but at least they will be given true information.

7 ❧ How to Live

You seem now to be closer to yourself than ever before. Trust yourself. Maybe you need just a break after the long work you have done. Your feelings will soon tell you what you need next. Nobody knows better what you need than your feelings when they eventually become your friends.

7 ❧ Breaking the Cycle

As you honestly want to explore the pain of your childhood, you should know that antidepressants may hinder your doing so. I hope you can find in my FAQ list (see "Articles" on my Web site) the help you need to find a therapist who can become your enlightened witness. As you succeeded in breaking the cycle of violence, you will certainly succeed in finding the right therapist. You have my best wishes.

8 ⤸ I Never See Anyone Express Emotions like Me

You seem to be recovering from the brainwashing of the twelve-step groups, and this indeed is not easy. But you are becoming a feeling person and this will give you real strength. You dare to feel and to have your *own* thoughts. Congratulations.

8 ⤸ To Please for Love

If you want to please, and to feel what you think that others expect you to feel, you are never yourself and thus you don't know yourself. We are not born to please; we are born to *be* who we are. We are entitled to have our own feelings and thoughts. If our parents refused us this right in our childhood, we must learn to reclaim it later as adults, otherwise we will never know who we are. We are our feelings. Rereading *The Drama* might help you to understand this.

12 ⤸ Forethought and Hindsight

If you were able to get in touch with your anger during this short time, the many dollars you had to pay were worthwhile. Prisons are full of people who kill but can't feel their anger, and they kill *because* they are unable to feel.

13 ⤸ The Angelic Role Model

You write: "I . . . usually always have wanted to understand them. I have been the angelic role model of this to my family and friends, but not as easily anymore." You need to stop this if you want to stay healthy.

15 ⪼ Thank You

Yes, goodness begets goodness, as you say—provided that it is authentic and not just pretend. You see it proven in the next generation, as in your case.

17 ⪼ Ritual Abuse

You are right: "People who write and create these movies seem to be totally unconscious to their own story, and have little understanding of what they're actually portraying and why." So what I am doing is writing time and again about *why* they are doing this, why they are showing monsters and brutal sex in their films and sell it as their "art," as a fantasy. Actually, it is the perversion they experienced as small children from their caregivers, which they have deleted from their memory. Children who watch these horror films must pay the price for the self-deception of the filmmakers.

19 ⪼ Some Answers

I will try to answer you as far as I can:
1. My FAQ list may help you to find the therapist who could enable you to feel.
2. You are right to mistrust hypnosis.
3. No, I don't encourage twelve-step programs.

19 ⌖ *Exploitation of Unmet Needs*

As a child, you get love from your parents if they are free to love you. If they are not (for whatever reason), you can't make them loving. However you may try, whatever you may do for them, it will never be enough. But as an adult, you can learn to recognize your actual needs, to take them seriously, to try to fulfill them. Then you will discover with surprise that you yourself can become the loving person you were always longing for.

20 ⌖ *Feeling like Shit*

Yes, it is very common that, after denouncing the deeds of their parents, people feel very badly at night, as if they were being punished. Because to see and condemn what the parents did was the worst sin, and children were often cruelly beaten if they saw too much. Feeling like shit is the memory of what probably happened many times, but this time you understand the connections and can no longer be forced to remain silent.

21 ⌖ *To Give Up the Illusion*

Everything you write makes sense to me. If your skin symptoms disappear, that will be wonderful, but if they still persist, maybe you need to give up the illusion that you can confront your mother and that you can "have an honest conversation and perhaps reconciliation."

22 & *I'd Like to Be Less Angry*

If you are angry, you have reasons to be angry, but you may be afraid to recognize them. When you feel your anger and realize what it triggers in your memory, it will leave you. Your body doesn't lie.

24 & *Like the Weather?*

No, denial is not just in the nature of things; otherwise we could not recover from our symptoms after having felt our truth. But it is, as you rightly say, common and ubiquitous. Almost everybody fears their parents who thus enjoy the absolute power they have over their own children. I hope that we can change this as we understand the catastrophic consequences of this dynamic (war, genocide, terrorism).

26 & *Feedback for* The Truth Will Set You Free

Yes, you seem to be living proof that "if we have the courage to speak out and claim our truth about our childhood trauma and subsequent reenactments throughout life, we no longer need be imprisoned by it because we are not in denial of it." For that reason, your body has recovered, and you will now be able to do the work you so much want to do.

MARCH 2007

5 ❧ *The Need to Be Listened To*

Not being heard can be a matter of life and death for a human being, right from the start. Imagine a newborn or a small baby whose only one language is crying. Only in this way can he say: I am hungry, I feel lonely, I need to be touched, etc. If his parents think that letting him cry will teach him to behave, his existence may be in mortal danger. As an adult, he may have very rich language but still be afraid that nobody is interested in knowing what he has to say, unless he has realized that there *do* exist people on this planet who are not exactly like his parents. Without therapy, parents rarely change in their eighties.

6 ❧ *Twelve-Step Programs of AA*

In my understanding, we can liberate ourselves from the effects of cruel parenting if we become free to feel our own authentic feelings, whatever they might tell us. But if our goal is to become loving and forgiving people who are loved by the Higher Power, we are obliged to cultivate the denial of our reality, which we learned to do as children—forgetting that it was exactly this denial that made us sick from the start.

6 ❧ *Finding Myself Again*

Your letter gives me hope that you will never again abandon the strong and rebellious girl that you have found; you like her and understand her. Probably it is all she needs now to live *her* own life, to learn for herself and to fulfill all the needs that will come along in the future.

7 ❧ Protecting Our Parents

Your observations are absolutely correct; you grew beyond your therapist. Why don't you look for another one if you still need a therapist? Don't let yourself be blinded again; you did it enough in your childhood. It is never, never, never right to spank a child. People do it only because they were beaten and still protect their parents.

9 ❧ Fear in the Spanked Child

In your honest and thoughtful letter, you write: "I realize it is the Fourth Commandment, public morals, and the fear of the little boy that is obstructing me." Three years ago I wrote a book to reveal the power of the Fourth Commandment and the public morals that forbid us to recognize the cruelty of our upbringing. But I do think that the last factor you mention above—the fear in the spanked child—is the most powerful obstruction to the truth. Even the fear of a small baby that we carry within us, sometimes for our whole life, can prevent us from admitting the truth about our parents. Because, with few exceptions, our parents were looking not for the truth but for power, which they obtained through our blindness. Thus most people have good reason to be scared by the suggestion that looking at their parents can help them with their health problems. But if they try, and find their symptoms disappearing they don't need to become convinced; they know why. However, these are rare exceptions. Almost all people on this planet think that children need to be smacked and to become obedient. They don't know the price of this ignorance.

9 ᐟ Creating Consciousness

Thank you so much for sending me the photos of your paintings. They are very expressive and powerful because they show authentic emotions. I can understand that talking about them makes you cry, but I hope that shame will disappear once you fully accept that you were the *victim* of cruelty and not its creator. What you create is *consciousness*, which is still very rare in the world of artists. Most of them don't want to know how they suffered in childhood, even if they express this suffering in art, but unconsciously.

11 ᐟ The Forbidden Feelings

You write: "My quality of life is so much better and so is my health. My back and muscles do not hurt as much, my chronic infections are gone, and my allergies are better. I still suffer from constipation, but I also have a long way to go before I can truly act out my new inner 'landscape.' I still find myself repressing my true feelings in many situations and choose not to act upon them because I'm still insecure in many ways." All this shows that you are on the right path to finding yourself. Nobody knows how long this path will be or how much time it will take to get rid of all the symptoms. But it is clear that you will succeed after all you have done. Your feelings know when they are ready to appear. Trust them.

20 ᧍ To Stand Up

You say: "When one can stand up to one's therapist, including their ignorance and abuse, one can truly stand up for oneself in the world." You are right, but only if the therapist represents parental ignorance. I hope that there are also therapists who are able to bear criticism.

APRIL 2007

3 ᧍ My Own Rage Scares Me

It is not by kicking soda bottles that you will liberate yourself from your rage, but by feeling and saying what hurts you and by understanding how you were hurt by your parents, how you were humiliated and tortured as a small defenseless child. You must admit that you have been carrying this rage your whole life but that now you are strong enough to defend yourself *with words*. Good luck!

4 ᧍ We Will Not Go Mad

No, we will not go mad if we dare to face our truth. Unfortunately, there are not too many counselors who help to do that.

4 ᧍ The Saved Life

I felt much moved by your story and the powerful self-portrait you sent me. Your letter confirms that healing *is* indeed possible if you decide to live with your truth. And your child *knows* it; his body knows that you are not lying. And I know it from your letter because everything you are saying here is coherent. I wish you and your family much luck.

5 ⌒ *I Will Forever Be Thankful for Your Research*

Thank you for your compliments, but you are giving me so much credit before reading my other books, written *after The Drama*. You write that your daughter is doing research into Parkinson's and Huntington's diseases. Are the scientists interested only in the description of the symptoms and in their genetic causes, or do they also show some interest in the emotional factors? Can research into Parkinson's disease be separated from the very obvious symptoms of fear that the bodies of these patients display?

5 ⌒ *Abusive Childhood Leads to Codependence, Another Kind of Prison*

You are asking: "Do I still feel lonely and unhappy because I feel chained to this depressed man, or is it my past to which I am still chained and from which I will never be free? Must children who were prisoners of abusive childhoods become and remain codependents as adults? Must I suffer physical symptoms if I stay for the sake of the kids? My knees are bothering me." These questions and your quotes from Nietzsche in my book show that you are coming very close to your essential question: Do I want to stay chained to my childhood until the end of my life, or are my knees asking me to open my eyes and become free of illusions so that I finally can live *my* life? You will become free if you decide to live with your truth.

6 ❧ *There Are Exceptions of Course*

I don't know any exception to the rule that *all* parents who deny the sufferings of their childhood and idolize their parents because they are (not without reason) too afraid of questioning their deeds will repeat what happened to them in a more or less cruel manner. But I hope that there are some who do dare to admit their truth or who were not abused at all. These kinds of parents are not compelled to pass on the cruelty they endured in childhood and denied in adulthood.

7 ❧ *The Body as Therapist*

You really got it! You write: "Since I have allowed myself to see this and the pain that comes along with it, the moment I lie to someone, my body immediately goes into a kind of panic sensation to let me know that it is not a good thing that you are about to do. This made a true believer out of me, that my body can inform me with this kind of message to keep me in line." You could say as well that your body is your most reliable therapist.

7 ❧ *Enemas*

Enemas are not a "necessary thing to do"; they confuse the natural and healthy work of the child's organs and make a "patient" out of a normal child. Besides, they produce shame and rage that are not allowed to be expressed and thus may become inaccessible in later life because the adult self thinks that the treatment was "necessary" and well meant. Actually, it is an abuse of power and often also a kind of sexual abuse.

8 ❧ *Is There a Cure for Depression?*

You are on the path to understanding more than your psychiatrist. The lack of serotonin has a cause, and this cause lies in your tragic childhood, but antidepressants will cover up your history. The knowledge of this story (an important part of your life) is the *real* key to your health. Your depression seems to ask you to face what happened *then*. You can leave a place only if you know where you have been. But you are still in your childhood without knowing it. I hope that reading *The Body Never Lies* will help you to make the right decision. Also read the article on depression and the FAQ list on my Web site.

12 ❧ *Surrealism: The Aftermath in the Minds of "Abused Children"?*

You can see it this way: society prefers to admire an artist who presents a "distorted mind" without a cause rather than acknowledge the suffering of a normal child who was submitted to incredible perversions by his or her parents (read the biographies of Surrealist painters).

13 ❧ *Ignorance*

I agree with you when you write that there is not enough creativity in the way parents and children are treated by therapists who are afraid of their own feelings. And I may add that these feelings are often the fears of a beaten child who was forced to suppress them. The adult therapist is not free then to listen and to see what happens to children in general and what happened to his or her clients in their childhood. Creativity means to be free from fear, to dare to have new experiences.

14 ♁ Poisonous Pedagogy in Primal Therapy

I totally disagree with the theory you cite and think, like you, that it indeed shows traces of poisonous pedagogy since rage and anger are condemned by all religions. However, these emotions are the most natural, healthy, and logical reactions to pain. Since these emotions are forbidden to children, they must be suppressed (in contrast to sadness, which is allowed). Neither in the family nor in school are these *important* and life-protecting emotions allowed to be felt and expressed in words. They thus stay blocked in our bodies, producing corporal symptoms in order to be heard. If they are taken seriously in adulthood, these emotions can be felt in therapy and then the symptoms may disappear, as they only occur in the first place as a nonverbal rebellion against injustice, cruelty, perversion, hypocrisy, lies, and a lack of love. In therapy they must be respected by a therapist who is not afraid of them. If clients mistakenly believe that their rage is only a defense against sadness, an illusion of "false power," they will—again—be unable to admit these emotions that block the functioning of their bodies, and the liberation of which would be healthy. Apparently, the *fear* of the little child that still lives within us penetrates many concepts of therapy. We prefer to stay good, obedient children rather than adults who can acknowledge the endless injustice they had to endure in their childhood and rebel against it.

15 ❧ Confronting Abusers

You seem to know what you want: to let the child in you speak under the protection of your adult self, to hear your voice and to honor your courage in the presence of your abusers. You also seem to be well prepared for the hurt you may confront again. But if you protect the child, you will overcome the pain. Anyway, you should be able to tell somebody how you feel after this confrontation.

15 ❧ Causes of Depression

You seem to know the causes of your depressions very well, but maybe you can't yet find access to the *feelings* of the little boy who had to care for his parents but was never cared for by them. I would suggest that you read my answer of yesterday, April 14, concerning the importance of feeling the *rage*.

18 ❧ Denying the Inner Child?

It is possible that most of us do not have any experience with the existence of the inner child because our fear of our parents didn't allow us to listen to his voice or understand his language, not even through body symptoms. Finally, we almost succeeded in killing it. But to declare then that *nobody* can listen to the inner child, and that it *doesn't exist* at all, is like saying that everybody must be blind because I have been made blind. This position is tragic but can be found very often. For that reason, our discovery of the tormented child and the messages it conveys through our bodies, of the suffering endured, is still neither shared nor understood by many. It is covered up by self-blame. But you seem to see through this mechanism, and once you act on it, you will find out much more.

18 ❧ Poisonous Pedagogy in the Spiritual Perspective?

It seems to be fashionable today to use the word "spirituality" when therapists reach the dead end of their promises. I must admit that I never understood the meaning or necessity of this word because it can easily be replaced by another one. If you say, for instance, that it is a feeling of being connected to an "All," to the whole universe, I imagine the feelings of a child who has been punished and isolated from the family before being forgiven and reincorporated into the (family) universe. Offering this outcome to a patient who dared to complain about his parents' abuse in childhood might be a good idea for some people who still feel guilty about their rage, but in my opinion this is not a healthy outcome and not a sign of successful therapy (see my answer of April 14).

18 ❧ Arthritis

Thank you for writing. What you write seems very coherent. Your arthritis will disappear as soon as you dare to feel your true emotions.

19 ❧ What Is Child Abuse?

You write: "It's as if I have no story, no inner life. Is this abuse?"
Is it not enough that you feel as if your inner life has been killed?
You will find your story and your inner life as soon as you dare to
feel rage about what has been done to you.

19 ❧ The Killings in Virginia

The killer was in psychiatric treatment and took antidepressants,
but his rage must have been stronger than all these drugs. Isn't it
amazing that, in the long discussion of this case, nobody raised
the question "Who did he hate so much and *why*?"

20 ❧ "Bad Genes"

Feeblemindedness seems to become more and more fashionable.
You can write to the journalist of the prestigious *New York Times*
and ask her why "nasty people," people with "bad genes," were so
frequently born in Germany thirty years before the Holocaust
to become Hitler's willing executors and why such people are
not to be found in Germany today. You will probably not get any
answer because she will not understand you, and she doesn't even
care about the answer. The right answer is: the Germans' brutal
upbringing thirty years before the Nazi regime, not "bad genes,"
produced the millions of adults who adored Hitler and helped him
to create a hell on earth. Their bodies knew the hell from their
childhood, but this knowledge was deeply repressed. They only
learned submission, and as adults they took revenge using entire
nations. This has nothing to do with the *New York Times* fairy tales

of "scientific" genes, but much to do with the laws of life. We could
see recently in Virginia how easily pent-up rage can destroy life.
Unfortunately, nobody seems to ask the most important question:
where does the hatred come from?

21 ⚭ Rage Released with an Enlightened Witness

Everything you write sounds true; now you *know* where you have
been all the time without knowing it. You can't lose this knowledge, and it will save you. The Virginia Tech story is a flight from
personal history with the help of drugs. Drugs only help to flee
and not to see. I am so glad that you dared to feel.

21 ⚭ The Stolen Life

I want to repeat here, in a different way, what I just wrote to
somebody else in another response: Not to be listened to in childhood teaches us not to listen to ourselves in adulthood. But your
depressive mood speaks a very clear language and you seem to be
listening now. When you once dare to do it, you will feel the rage
about what you had to endure, and it is this rage and the knowledge
that it brings that will make the difference.

26 ⚭ The Internal Critical Voice

All my books deal with these internal voices. If you take time
to read them, they may help you; I can't repeat here what I have
already written. It is *not* easy to blame the parents, not at all,
because it scares us—we expect to be punished. Blaming oneself

is easier. But the price we pay might be our illness, or that of our children.

26 ~ *Rage*

Your rage can become the door to your actual life. Try to feel it as strongly and clearly as possible, then, *not before*, try to understand its cause. Similar situations from the past will soon come to your mind. Now you can see and feel what the child was forbidden to see; now you can really, and not only intellectually, understand what she had to endure in silence. The more you do this, the more you will become grounded in yourself, in your history, in your reality, and the more clearly you will come to know what you *need* and what you want to do to be able to live your own life instead of living the life of a person who is *not you*.

28 ~ *Protecting My Child*

You dared to feel, you dared to think, and you took action so that you don't need to hate your child for what your father did. The strong feeling of rage showed you how to care for yourself, what you needed to do to feel better. You will be able to use this experience time and again when the rage comes up; the rage will show you what you need at that given moment to feel comfortable in your "skin." This is how good therapy works. Since you also dared to consciously feel and understand the fear of the child before you acted as an adult, you know that *this* fear doesn't indicate a danger for you now. But it did then for the child. Now you will protect this child from abuse.

MAY 2007

4 ᒷ The First Step to the Truth

Your moving letter shows that you *are* already living the truth; it is
normal that you can't stay there all the time, because it is extremely
painful to be "on the cross of parental needs for love." I hope that
one day you will be able to leave this cross and take care of the
small, abused girl that has been waiting for your attention, your
compassion, and your love for such a long time. I wish you the
courage to do so.

4 ᒷ Seeing Through Lies

You *are* on the right path. You need time. The courage to say *no*
will come with more knowledge. Most people have neither your
courage nor your knowledge. They think what they were made to
think when they were small: that children have to obey, that by
spanking them you can teach them to become a nice person, that
children need "limits," etc. You have already made a big step if you
can see through all these lies.

4 ᒷ I Am Tired of Pretending

It is not easy to suddenly live with the truth, but you see that your
body responds with gratitude. I wish you the courage to continue
and not to give up.

6 ⤸ The Courage to See

You can recover from your disease if you find the courage to see what your parents did to the small child you once were and to feel your suppressed rage. With your symptoms you protect your parents from blame and yourself from the expected punishment. Once you no longer do that, your symptoms will disappear because their function will no longer be needed.

8 ⤸ Hope

You write that my books solidified your faith in your own judgment and your trust in your body. This is exactly what I hope to do with everything I have been writing. I don't want people just to believe in what I am writing, I want them to prove everything they read through their own lives. It is rather unusual that you are able to do it at such a young age—you can save your future, your life.

9 ⤸ Mother's Day

You want me to answer the questions that your body tries to answer you. Maybe it will try as long as your mother is alive so that you can see how far your memories are correct. Some months ago you wrote that you were never beaten, but now you have a new memory. That is not unusual when we are ready to give up our denial. You can benefit now from asking your mother questions and listening to her answers; this will make you more compassionate with the small boy who was forced to laugh when he needed to cry. Now take the liberty to feel your truth.

12 ❧ Question of a Therapist

You are a therapist and you have read the three books I wrote first. Now, the only question that you want me to answer is the time it took to write them. I wrote *The Drama* in a few weeks, but it was based on twenty years of therapeutic experience.

12 ❧ Sexual Abuse and Memory

The knowledge of your body and your dreams *are* your memories. They should allow you to feel the rage about your terrible abuse and it is this rage that will set you free.

13 ❧ Activities in Poland

I opened your Web site and was impressed by your serious engagement and skillful organization of the material you want to pass on to others. This is hard work, I know; most people want to avoid knowing what their body knows but what their consciousness has deeply repressed and denied. It is not easy to talk to them about abusive childhoods. However, sooner or later, their lives will force them to confront their truth and then—if not yet misled by pharmacy—they will benefit from your Web site. I wish you courage to continue your important work for the truth.

18 ❧ Awakening

I hope that many people will read and reread your letter, because it tells so clearly what good therapy is all about. There is nothing I could add to your text; every sentence speaks the truth of your own experience, and this is more valuable than books could ever be.

26 ◌ *Nearly Swept Away*

I am happy that *The Drama* helped you to touch your feelings. My most recent books will help you to stay with your decision to love the mistreated child you once were and not to blame yourself for what others have done. As soon as you are ready to *see* what has happened, your body will no longer need to make you aware of your truth through insomnia and depression.

28 ◌ *Denying Child Abuse*

You are absolutely right in what you have written. The lack of interest in child abuse at universities shows that we are all formerly battered children who are still, even as grown-ups, afraid of the next blow if we open our mouths.

30 ◌ *Born with Hope*

Your letter seems to be written out of your own profound experience. You write: "The depression and anxiety are the consequences of realizing my grandiose dreams won't come true. But the feelings of powerlessness, worthlessness, guilt, and hopelessness are the feelings of an abused child. I refuse to hold onto those feelings. They were real, those were the feelings any human child would have when held captive by cruel adults. But I won't have them now, they will kill me, and I won't let them. I was born with love for myself and others and I won't abandon it. I've noticed that grandiose people who achieve their goals of fame and fortune are often unhappy, drug addicts, alcoholics, etc. Public success does not lead to happiness. How many examples do we need?" You are so right, especially when you say that we are born with the ability to love ourselves and to hope. This ability is so often damaged in us by abusing parents, but we can regain it. I fully agree: public success is an illusion of happiness, often paid for with our health, and it doesn't nurture us. Instead, love for the tormented child we once were gives us the knowledge of who we are and what we actually need, so we become strong enough to fulfill these needs. In this way we maintain hope.

31 ❧ Seing Without Blinders

You write: "Sharing your knowledge and experiences has helped me to open my eyes, heart, and body to understand about my personal life." The more you open your eyes to the tormented child you once were, the more you will see all the scandalous events around you; but you will also find the courage to speak up, as you did here.

JUNE 2007
1 ❧ On Healing

With very strong feelings, it is still better not to be alone, to have a good, understanding witness. But you are right, there is plenty of other work that you can do alone—for instance, writing letters that you will not send, recognizing in this way how your parents treated you and what impact this had on you. Nobody can find this out better than you yourself. The more you see the damage done to you, the more you begin to love the small boy who had to endure it, silently, without any help.

1 ⌇ Ghosts from the Nursery: Tracing the Roots of Violence

I know the book and both of its authors whom I met in New York in 1998. I loved their book; it is brave, honest, very informative, and written from the heart. I mention it repeatedly in my book *The Truth Will Set You Free*, and publish with pleasure your letter and the review. I would like to add that by abusing and neglecting children, we not only produce unhappy children and adults but also many future child abusers. This dynamic of passing on cruelty is still unmentioned, ignored, or denied by most authors.

2 ⌇ *Seeing the Parents as the Problem*

Of course, the parents are the problem, not the children. But nobody wants to understand that parents are not free to give their children emotional support if they are stuck in their fear of their own parents and don't dare to question their cruel behavior. Out of this fear, they repeat the cruelties to which they were subjected in their own childhoods.

3 ⌇ *The Effects of Parental Humiliation*

Your suspicion is absolutely correct. Acknowledging this is the first step to healing. The next would be to acknowledge the huge rage that has been accumulating in the body for such a long time, then to express it by doing what you always wanted but were not allowed: to write, to speak up, to protect the small tortured boy who lives in fear of being hurt again. Today nobody can hurt you again, unless you let them do it. I wish you the strength and the courage to take your life in *your* hands, away from the power of your father.

4 ✑ A Bunch of Angry Letters

You got it! Write, write, write your "bunch of angry letters," as many as you need. Read them several days later and *then* decide whether you will send them. Writing and feeling your rage will lessen your fear; it will give you the strength and the wisdom that you need to make this decision, because then you will only want to express yourself, not to make new troubles. And the *felt* and *understood* anger doesn't stay forever.

5 ✑ Anger Is One of My Feelings

You write: "I am listening to my anger now as well. I have more information since doing that and I already feel less angry! What a gift it is to be able to understand the communication of my anger when others thought it was something that I should get rid of! I knew that I was right, and I am very glad that I stood my ground. I will never, ever again allow someone else to tell me what things I should feel and what things I should not feel. My feelings are *mine*. They belong to me and I will not let anyone take away anything of mine anymore." I think that with this insight and experience you can't be lost again; you won't become a target of addiction again for a long time. Your feelings will inform you at the moment when you are about to damage yourself, and they will help you to choose what is right and healthy for you.

5 ⌁ My Body Rebels

Ask your body why it rebels. If you hate your mother because she was so cruel to you, why do you think you must help her, especially if she already gets help from your brother, whom she may have treated differently? Probably your body can't understand this; it insists on your truth. How can you relax if you force yourself to do something that you don't want to do? Read the letter we are publishing today about "feelings," and my answer. That may encourage you to listen to your symptoms and to respect their clear message.

6 ⌁ To Stand Up for the Future

I am so glad about your "standing up when the others sat," and about your clear insight that child abuse is not *only* a family matter. In my opinion, it is also the industry, with the permission of the whole society, of all governments, and of all religions, that produces new child abusers.

7 ⌁ If the Bible Was Against Beating Children

I agree with you completely. Actually, you succeeded in putting my main message into six lines, and I hope that you find a way to spread it widely. I have written thirteen books by now, and it is still unusual to find somebody who understands the last few words in your letter. What can we do to make it clear that by hitting children we are producing abusers?

8 ⦵ *Enlightened Witness*

You have read five books written by me, and you ask me to write about how people can become more empathic. If all my thirteen books were unable to teach empathy, it could mean that feeling empathy for children is not teachable once the capacity for it has been destroyed by child abuse and a complete lack of compassion.

12 ⦵ *Ferenczi's Prison*

I totally agree with you when you write: "They [Sándor Ferenczi and Sigmund Freud] were indeed prisoners of their heads. They well cemented their childhood feelings with the help of their intellects and rather complex theories." I hope that you eventually find a therapist who is free to feel indignation. Have you read my article on this topic? Once you can *feel* the torture children so often have to endure from their parents, you can no longer be fooled by theories. You know that they do nothing other than keep the fear of the tormented child inside. Most people do the same all the time.

14 ⦵ *Your Book Really Touched Me*

You describe yourself as high-functioning, and this might have been your "successful" way of escaping depression—but also of escaping your history and your understandable pain. I can thus imagine that my books will touch you and inspire you to feel emotions you have never dared to feel before. They may make you aware of having had these emotions since your early days. Try to trust them; they will tell you the story of the very little girl that needs your compassion and understanding for her plight and loneliness. And you will no longer want to escape her because you have learned to love and protect her. I wish you the courage you need to meet her.

14 ⚭ *Informing Parents*

I don't hold conferences, but you can learn from me if you carefully read the articles and interviews on my Web site. All my books are also available in Spanish. It is a pleasure to learn that you want to inform parents about the needs of their children. This work is very important because most parents merely repeat what they have learned as children—spanking.

14 ⚭ *Spanking as Sexual Abuse*

Yes, I agree with you, this is a double taboo. But you are right to keep trying to make people aware of their fear by writing to them about what you know and expecting responses. If everybody stays silent, nothing will ever change. Thank you for your courage, for seeing the truth and trying to make it seen.

15 ⚭ *To Find Our True Needs*

You are right: Living with the truth of our history, and finally rebelling against the cruelty endured, gives us the sense and the power to understand our true needs and to fulfill them. How did you find out that your father abused you sexually as a baby?

16 ᘾ Thomas Gordon's Parent Effectiveness Training

Thomas Gordon's advice concerning a "family conference" is excellent and could save our society if it was used everywhere. Also, the ideas of Marshall Rosenberg about nonviolent communication are very helpful. But both were published more then thirty years ago and are still not used by the majority of parents. Why? Because parents who were severely mistreated in their childhood, and who deny these facts, are unconsciously compelled to repeat that damage on their children. Many of them are not motivated to have children who are free and healthy, for this would reveal to them the pain of their own upbringing that they try not to feel. Instead, they make their children feel it. The idea of a free child already scares them. I thus think that to be able to help our child we must get in touch with our repressed feelings concerning our own history of mistreatment. Parents who have done this can enormously benefit from Gordon and Rosenberg; also, all parents who were brought up without violence. Here they can find much important information and are free to use it. People who deny the pain of their childhood are rarely free to understand anything but violence. However, I have always supported Gordon and am glad that you wrote about him and described your experience.

16 ⌖ *Forgiveness*

I was very moved by your letter. You write: "I no longer feel emotionally blind. I finally am starting to feel things I never allowed myself to feel." Your whole letter shows that you are speaking the truth. I wish you the courage you need to be able to face your history, and I am sure that this work will give you all you need to feel well in this world and to help others without being damaged by them.

18 ⌖ *Government-Sponsored Child Abuse*

I read your message, and it contains important information indeed; but you are not the first person to report shocking facts concerning organized child abuse. Every day we receive plenty of such information. Although I can't do more than to write, I am glad that there are people like you who are able to see what others so easily overlook. I thus hope that you will find a way to take *effective* action and inform the ignorant people in power, instead of writing to somebody like me who is well informed but has not the slightest means to change the state of affairs. I can assure you that I will do everything that I feel I need to do and *can* do on my own but not more.

19 ⌖ *Vicious Circles of Contempt*

Could it be that your deepest, most justified contempt is the contempt the intelligent small boy holds for his sadistic parents who pitilessly tortured their child? But it was then very dangerous to show or even to *have* these feelings. They could never be felt; they had to be suppressed. Today they want to be acknowledged by the conscious adult you are becoming, and they are, fortunately, at first directed to people who will not punish you, because they love you. To feel all these awful feelings, you have to feel safe. When you can feel the fear of the small boy, you can tell him that he is now no longer in danger and help him to direct his contempt toward your parents, who fully deserve it.

20 ❧ My Experience as a Child Victim and as an Adult Writer

You write in your beautiful, strong, and true letter: "I am floating alone, lost in an amorphous universe of family, a family wherein I didn't merely do wrong; I was wrong. I didn't make mistakes; I was the mistake." No, you were *not*; you are a wonderful, very talented author and an honest person. But your family was a mistake— more than that, your family was criminal. I think that you must publish your story, but I can imagine why people are so afraid of publishing it. It reminds them of their own stories that they don't dare to confront. I had similar experiences: Many of my books were bought and published in different countries, but in some of them publishers bought the rights more than ten years ago and yet have never published the books, nor have they given back the rights so that someone else could publish them. Your book needs to be fully appreciated. And you need your own courage to come out of your parents' office and to say: "I am not going to spare you my truth, I hated you for what you did and I don't owe you any lies about love. Ever."

26 ❧ To Open the Eyes

If you can benefit so much from *The Drama*, you may find much more information in my more recent books. Maybe you will find the therapist you are looking for when you use my FAQ list to prepare your questions for the first interview. We have no lists of therapists. In any case, today I no longer recommend psychoanalysts, because I feel that, unfortunately, they side with the adult and not with the child, as Freud did in his theories and his treatments. To recover from the tragic effects of child abuse, we need a well-informed witness who is not protecting the abusive parents.

JULY 2007

1 ❧ Re: No Idea How Bad It May Have Been— Thursday, June 14, 2007

You should never do "the last thing that you would actually want to do"—even if a hundred counselors say that you should. Rather you should ask your body what it wants you to do.

4 ❧ Book-Writing

Just write, and have fun, and feel that you are always yourself without wanting to please anybody. Just say what feels right to you and your body, according to your own experience. Should it feel betrayed, your body will tell you.

4 ⌾ *Fear of Achieving*

Never being praised as a child is very intimidating. Your strong emotional reaction to the letter of June 3 may help you to feel the rage of the child who was never supported in what was important to him. I wish you the courage to feel this rage and to give your child the support he now needs from you.

5 ⌾ *Diary I*

It is *never* too late to get in touch with your history and your true feelings. The diary is a good place to start. It can also be helpful to write letters to your parents telling them how you are still suffering from what they did. You must not send these letters at the moment, but writing to them may release your feelings and the rage that is a normal reaction to abuse, but was withheld for such a long time at the cost of your health. Try to read my book *The Body Never Lies*.

6 ⌾ *Diary II*

Thanks so much for your response; I would be glad to hear in a few months how you have succeeded with your work. Now you seem to have already become the enlightened witness to the child you once were, and this is certainly much better than going to confusing therapists who fear their own memories and their suppressed rage.

7 ᘓ Question About a Therapist

Ask your own feelings and don't let them be fooled. Don't you feel betrayed? The contract with a therapist says that the helplessness, the love and trust of the client, should *never* be exploited for the needs of the therapist. Otherwise the story of one's childhood abuse is repeated instead of being felt with rage, and rejected in therapy. Abuse continues to be tolerated and seen as normal. It is common, indeed, but it is *not* right. You still seem to protect your therapist from your anger, just as you probably protect your parents. When you start to protect *yourself* by *seeing* what has been done to you, you will no longer need my answers. *You* will become the expert.

7 ᘓ Letters to Parents

You seem to have found a kind of enlightened witness, and I think that anything is okay if it helps you to feel and to learn to use your voice. At least these are your words. By listening many times, you will become used to your truth, which at first seemed absolutely unbelievable. This can be more helpful than anything an old-fashioned therapist can do for you today.

8 ᘓ My Body Is Shouting About Something

Maybe your body was "shouting" about "something that had happened the day before." Instead of speculating about the badness of human beings, ask the body (the child) what actually made her furious. It will answer you.

9 ↷ What My Body Is Shouting About

You've got the right answer; your body is enraged because the incident in the hospital triggered your memory. Your parents betrayed
you and robbed you of your consciousness, so that you were unable
to see what they did and protest against their deeds. You were a
child; there was nothing you could do to defend yourself. Now the
arthritis tells you how furious you are about this violation and the
silence of your therapist. The pain in the body wants to help you,
to make you aware of your feelings. Try to feel them, and don't
protect your father in any way. What he did was a crime. Maybe
you can write and fully express your feelings, all of them; then the
pain in your body will leave.

10 ↷ The Global Denial

You are so right: Attachment to abusive parents can be very destructive, and self-destructive, and it is worse that this truth is rarely
understood and mostly denied out of fear of punishment. All religions protect the parents and cultivate the blindness and submission
of the child. As a result, doctors are not allowed to recognize the
true reasons for the illnesses they are confronted with. This global
denial leads to a madness that seems "normal" because it is never
questioned and is strongly supported by religious authorities.

10 ↷ Dangerous "Friends"

I think that your conclusions are absolutely correct. The way your
"friend" tried to impose her "opinions" (or rather her fears) on you

shows how she might have done the same with her small child. Fortunately, you are no longer blind, and you are no longer dependent on mortifying friends. You asked us not to publish your last letter and we respected your wish. But maybe you could write a shorter version, including your dialogue with the limb and its answer to you. I think that this story could encourage some readers to try the same. They are as scared as you are about daring to feel differently from the way they were told was "right," but the help and the wisdom of the body is so surprising and so convincing in your history. You can recall it again and again, and work with this memory to soothe your fear. It will work, but only if you don't let your "friends" intimidate and contaminate you.

11 ҽ *Abused Abusers*

One repeats with one's children the cruelties endured in one's own childhood only as long as one denies that one was treated cruelly. If you know your history and don't protect your parents (by saying that everybody *must* [?] be cruel), you will never abuse your child. You can only have empathy for his or her emotional needs if your feelings are not blocked through denial. To understand what I am saying here, you can read my articles on my Web site or, if you don't have enough time, you can just read the first page of the Web site.

11 ҽ *Stuck*

Your pity for your mother is absolutely comprehensible, but it seems to completely swallow the empathy you need for the suffering of the small child who has become the protector of the mother without having a protector himself. It *is* now possible for you, as an adult, to become this witness, to develop compassion for the overburdened child you once were.

12 ↝ *How I Help Myself*

Your letter will give other people ideas about how they can help themselves to understand the language of their bodies. You are especially creative in finding this language, a kind of pioneer, but others will follow your example in their own way as soon as they get rid of their fear of being punished for discovering the truth. This danger no longer exists—we are free to know; but in our childhood we were not, so the fear may remain. However, we can become free of this fear if we accept that the dialogue with the body really works.

13 ↝ *Irrational Side of Our Lives*

You write: "I think what I like most about your work, what was so powerful for me, was the idea that even the irrational side of our lives can be understood and explained." I think that what seems irrational to us is the disguised version of our story that we deny because it is so painful. Once people find the courage to face their stories and to feel how terribly they suffered in their childhood, their behavior, fears, and addictions no longer seem irrational; they reveal themselves as *logical* consequences of abuse endured. Each life is unique, and nothing is irrational if we dare to see the reality of even a single childhood. Unfortunately, this is seldom done in all the recovery programs that offer behavioral, religious or "spiritual" ways to "overcome" the abuse; without being forced to see and recognize the cruelty of one's own parents, participants cannot face and feel their own reality.

13 ⌖ Nightmares

You write: "The nightmares always had the same theme: someone was about to kill me or I was caught in a small space between four walls without an escape. Waking up in the middle of the nightmare was extremely fearful and terrifying. My husband told me at one of these occasions that I was screaming, 'Mummy, mummy' don't put me in the closet.' " Your dreams, and the information from your husband, clearly show that your body *knows* what happened to you at a very early time of your life: you were put into the closet (!). To feel what this was like for a small child is more than one can imagine, so to deny it sometimes seems like the only way to survive. You need time to get in touch with these terrible feelings of fear, rejection, hurt, and despair. But you seem to have the courage, and you are willing to come to know your history and no longer deny it. So you will succeed in doing it, step by step, because now you are no longer in danger, unless you protect your perpetrators by your denial. The nightmares want to help you to eventually *believe* and take seriously what your body tells you.

14 ⌖ Psychogenic Hearing Loss

I know that many women suffering from bulimia report that they were sexually abused, but I have never heard about it causing hearing loss.

14 & *Truth Concealed Causes Child's Suffering*

It is up to you to recognize what your daughter needs to know from you at the moment: you must not impose *your* needs on her in an attempt to "fix" her again. Be open and honest to her questions, as this will mean much to her. But forcing her to ask questions that she doesn't have is you imposing your needs on her.

17 & *Psychosomatic Symptoms and Working Through the Pain I*

Were you beaten in your childhood? Can you remember these incidents? Were the beatings painful? Was it your father, your mother, or both who punished you? For which deed were you punished? What can you remember from this time? Can you cry?

17 & *Psychosomatic Symptoms and Working Through the Pain II*

Now you have described everything you need to know in order to liberate yourself from all your physical pain. The problem is that *you don't want to know* all this, and for that reason you make your body suffer. It is understandable that, having had a father like yours, your fear of being killed if you show rage is great. So you have kept your rage in your body for twenty-four years, and it is no wonder that this rage produces terrible physical pain. You have no choice other than to *feel* this fear and rage in order to liberate your body from this poison. Today, your father can't do anything else to you unless you allow him to kill you. It is important that you understand this. Now you are no longer in danger; you are free to hate him for what he has done, and you have no other choice but to feel your rage so you can save your life. Your therapist seems to understand this, but he must be able to hold your body when you are screaming at your father and telling him that he almost killed you when you were a small child and that this is a crime. Repeat it *many* times, in the arms of your therapist, and you will see that you will eventually feel your tremendous rage. Scream out your justified rage and the pain of your wounded soul, and the pain of your body will leave you. Do not take any drugs or medication.

19 ❧ Is Public Exposure Dangerous?

I wrote this in a footnote about fifteen years ago when this kind of exposure was very rare. It was then very often met with total misunderstanding and a lack of empathy. For the authors of such books, the cold or even rejecting reactions could be very hurtful and the cause of new traumas. I wouldn't write this note today because I think (or hope at least) that readers and reviewers of autobiographic books dealing with their own abuse endured in childhood are better informed, and that the issue is more discussed today. But it is still very common to ridicule people who describe their plight as children and accuse them of self-pity, because this is what most people learned to do during their own childhood. They learned to side with the abusive parents and are thus afraid of siding with the child.

19 ❧ A Horrific Memory Came Up Last Night!

You don't need medication—it is harmful. Now you can feel what happened to you because you have this important memory that makes you aware of your story. It is amazing, but effective therapy works exactly this way: feeling your extreme weakness makes you strong. And suddenly you want to join a rock group. Yes, why not? Without any doubt, it is right if it eventually brings you fun.

20 ⟨e⟩ *Emotional Honesty— Overcoming Brain Damage*

If you read and understand my book *The Truth Will Set You Free: Overcoming Emotional Blindness*, you will see why there is no contradiction, and how the adult can get rid of his brain damage. We have empirical proof, which you can find on these pages, that people can experience the rage they have withheld their whole lives and suppressed in their bodies, getting rid of their symptoms as they become aware of what has been done to them. This happens when they succeed in overcoming their fear of losing their parents' "love" if they are true to themselves, if they are emotionally honest and show their legitimate rage or criticism. Most people don't take this risk, remaining their whole life in fear of their childhood. If children are forbidden to show their strongest emotions, such as rage, they may (wrongly) believe their whole lives that withholding them guarantees them the love of their parents. In one of your postings you have also written that you can't criticize your mother because you don't want to lose her love. This conviction may be the result of the early brain damage, which can, however, be undone by taking advantage of being adult and taking the liberty to express authentic feelings.

21 ⚭ The Paths to Yourself

You have succeeded in coming to understand your feelings, as well as respecting them. I thus don't understand why you write, "Today is my mother's birthday and I've decided to see her after many arguments. But my feelings are no good in relation to her and my memories. I feel responsible for keeping some relationship between my daughter and my mother, but I know that my mother is neither honest with me nor with her." Why do you feel responsibility for allowing your daughter to have a relationship with a grandmother who is not honest, neither with you nor with her? Don't you need to protect your daughter? You also write, "My body is telling me about my real feelings through some skin allergy on my fingers, so I decided that I needed to write this letter." Your symptoms are a language: ask your body what it is telling you. Did you need to write to me so that your truth could be taken seriously? I do it of course, but your body calls for *your* compassion above all. I am sure that you will learn this. You are on the best path to helping yourself.

21 ⚭ Killing the True Self

We *can* learn to give up compassion for somebody who abused us and stopped us from living our true emotions, our *true self*. This is like killing a person.

24 ⚭ My Brother Denies the Truth

It is a problem that many people have, and I can empathize with you. You have trouble believing that your parents were so cruel; you hope and hope that your memory is wrong, that your emotions are fooling you, but you want to be honest with yourself and eventually you see. There is no escape from the truth, your body doesn't let you lie. Then, as a last hope, you suppose that the person who also suffered from the same parents, who knows your reality, will confirm your truth, will say: Yes, I know that you are right. But he doesn't do it; he does not have your courage and your honesty. If he had them, he would not have punished you in the same way as he had been punished. You can't change him; you can't force him to do the hard work if he doesn't want to. You must let him be how he is. It may be very painful for you; his denial may trigger your rage about what he did to you when you were a small child without protection. I think, instead of having pity for your brother, express your long-withheld rage and write him about how you felt and still feel about being tortured by him sadistically. If you try to help *him* now by protecting him from your rage, which he deserves, you will betray yourself and abandon yourself like you may have done in your childhood. You know that your body would have to pay the bill for this self-betrayal.

25 ❧ Powerless

Even physical abuse in schools is not against the law in twenty-one states of the United States. Out of 192 members of the United Nations, only 19 (mostly European countries) have a law that forbids the corporal punishment of children. I can understand your feelings of powerlessness and do of course share them. Unfortunately, for politicians and the pope this doesn't seem to be an "issue." The information that spanking small children during the time when their brains are developing leaves them with lingering destructive effects does not hold their interest at all. It does not motivate them to take any action.

26 ⟆ Creative Remembering, or Just Craziness?

You know very well that you are not crazy and not to blame, and what your mother wants is to blame you instead of your father. But the small child could not fathom the truth; she could not believe that her father was a criminal and that both parents betrayed her. So you have protected them your whole life, but you wrote novels because the truth wanted to be acknowledged. Now you, the adult, will have the courage to know, to read the novels and to know that they tell you the truth of what you had to endure all alone, as a very small girl, without any protection. Nobody invents horror. You are honest and you no longer want to betray yourself. Why should you? Because that is what your mother wants? But should you lie to yourself so that she can live with her lies? It is your life and you need your truth. Everything you write here shows this need. Trust your memories, trust your novels; reading them can be a very relieving experience. The pain of truth was unbearable for the child, but now it will be liberating for you as an adult. It was of course creative of your child to tell her story through novels, and she absolutely needs to be heard. The first and the most empathic listener should be *you*. Your mother never wanted to see the truth of your plight; it was very mean of her to blame you for what your father had done. They both should be ashamed for their total lack of courage and honesty.

26 ☙ I Didn't Know Who I Was

It is impossible for a child who endured so much abuse and rape, who was constantly used for the pleasure of others without being respected and without being allowed to show her feelings of rage and disgust, to know *who she is*. She was constantly forced to suppress her feelings, so how can she come to know herself? I am glad that my books "opened your eyes and your heart," as you write, and that they could bring you in touch with your feelings, because without them you can't be an effective psychotherapist. You can't understand others if you don't know yourself. I wish you the courage to continue this work.

26 ☙ Connected to Myself

Your optimistic reaction to my answer shows your potential for recovery and also what your depression is telling you: "You are protecting your family from your rage so you can feel generous and can hope to be eventually loved by them for your generosity." This "strategy" is dictated by the agonizing fear of the small boy, fully dependent on his parents and siblings. But now you don't have to be emotionally dependent on them if you don't want to be. Once you have realized this, you can (and you have the right to) refuse playing the role of a scapegoat—the role they imposed upon you when you were totally defenseless. Then the depression will leave you for good, and you will be free to show your true feelings without needing to protect anybody from them. Because your feelings of rage and contempt are justified after all, they should no longer poison your body or confuse your mind.

29 ❧ Sister Behaves like Abusive Father

You cannot change your sister. Why don't you listen to your feel-ings, which clearly indicate that you feel better when you have no contact with her? Nobody can force you to see her. As a child, you were dependent on your parents even if they were abusive, but as an adult you can say *no*.

31 ❧ Your Own Models

You write: "Being a male in western culture is fraught with dif-ficulties. While males are supposed to be stoic and unemotional in this culture, I find it hard to conform to this type of stereotypical behavior." Why should you conform to this stereotype? If you don't find role models you like, you can create them. Anyway, what you yourself create will give you more fun than what you will find in books and whatever you do without fun is annoying.

AUGUST 2007
4 ❧ After the Knowledge, What?

You write about wanting "to re-create and recover the sense of security, wonder, and power I once had." I don't understand how you ever had it if you grew up with a detached mother and an alco-holic father who (as you felt) wanted to kill you. Can you explain this contradiction?

4 ❧ Is Contemporary Psychoanalytic Thought Just Another Wolf in Sheep's Clothing?

You seem to be on the right track. No, I have not changed my opinion on psychoanalysts and self-psychologists and think today, even more strongly than before, that they avoid confronting the issue of child abuse. I think confrontation is absolutely unavoidable if "empathy" is to be more than just a nice word. Words are often used to pretend something that doesn't exist. The Church loves to use the word "compassion," but allows children to be beaten so that God can "find pleasure in them." For two thousand years *nobody* protested against this practice. As most of us were beaten children, we have not learned to have empathy with ourselves or with the plight of other children. We learned to deny our pain to survive, but this is a big handicap for a therapist. Heinz Kohut tried at first to open our eyes and hearts to what a child has to endure, but he felt very isolated in the psychoanalytic community. He returned to traditional concepts at the end of his life, the concepts that Freud invented when he himself suffered from society's rejection after he had disclosed the sexual abuse by parents. As soon as he declared that patients talk only about their fantasies and not about real events, he found a huge number of followers who still seem very stable in their denial of the reality of child abuse. To sufficiently answer your very important question I would need to repeat what I have written extensively elsewhere. Try to read the article on indignation on my Web site (Dr. Lachman, whom I mention there, is actually a self-psychologist) as well as the last articles on my concept of therapy.

4 ⤷ *Schizophrenic Families*

I agree with everything you write. It is true that the families of
incest victims have much in common with families of schizophren-
ics; in both it is forbidden to see the truth. Because families like
that seem to be much more common than healthy ones, we have
trouble being heard when we write and say the truth. Almost
everything R. D. Laing wrote was right, but psychiatrists of today
hardly mention him. We must conclude perhaps that they also
learned very early to deny their truth and are afraid of getting in
touch with it. So instead of listening to the patients and their stories, they make them silent and even more confused by giving them
drugs. Also, politicians, journalists, and teachers seem to be very
scared by memories of their own histories when we write about
what we found out thanks to our feelings. I can only congratulate
you on liberating yourself from this conspiracy of lies and making
your life, and above all your body, feel healthier now. Do you know
the story of the Freyd family who invented *false memory syndrome*
after their daughter talked about being sexually abused by her
father? You can find Jennifer Freyd's book on the Internet.

5 ⤷ *Arthritis and Anger*

Your clarity is wonderful. You don't deserve to live in such a prison.
It is understandable that your body rebels. It seems to say: You can't
live this way; you must make a decision. Can it be that you will
find the outcome if you allow yourself to feel the rage of the small
girl toward your father, whom you still seem to protect? The child
could not leave, but the adult has options that she doesn't see as
long as she is blocked by the feelings of her childhood.

5 ℮ An Artist's Autobiography

You are right: child abuse is not a private matter. For that reason I fully agree with you that it should be revealed and not covered by silence. However, the grown-up children are usually hated by society when they disclose the brutality of their parents in public, because most people were battered children; even as adults, they are afraid to see the truth and to be punished for seeing it. We must work against this fear, and we are doing this here.

6 ℮ Shaky but Real

Your answer makes much sense, except for this sentence: "After that I finally accepted the notion that I had been abused, and began the exploration of myself, knowing that perhaps my messed-up life, and who I was, was not altogether my fault." I would suggest that you take out the word "altogether." You were terribly abused and it was *not at all* your fault.

6 ℮ Birth Trauma and Psychedelics

I don't know of any other issue that is so feared and so avoided as the story of our own abuse suffered in childhood, the pain of being exploited, humiliated, hated, and terrorized by people whom we loved, trusted, and needed to survive. So we had to learn *not to see* what happened to us, and most people would prefer to do anything else rather than face the very painful truth of their story, even if they know that facing it could help them with their health problems. For that reason you can find a huge amount of suggestions of what you can do *instead* of emotionally acknowledging how you were treated by your parents when you were a small, defenseless child. If you really *want* to do this work, you don't need drugs, because the knowledge of everything you had to endure is stored up in your body. I am not an expert for giving you advice about all these ways of avoiding the most terrible pain. I can only say that the truth can't be replaced, but it *can be felt* if you are no longer afraid of your parents. Now they are no longer dangerous to the adult you have become.

6 ☙ Confused

You write: "But for some reason, after the conversations with my mother, I feel very confused. There is still anger in me at the mother she once was, but I find it difficult to be angry at the mother she is now, because she changed so much. I feel I am losing direction in these contradictions." Your body doesn't ask you to be angry at how your mother is now, but it needs you to feel consciously what you didn't dare to feel when you were the defenseless child, abused by others, and she didn't defend you. The small child you were suppressed his rage within his body, and it is from there (instead of in your mind) that you can feel your anger originating. Even if your mother is now an angel, this does not change the fact that your body contains the memory of being abused and that you are constantly afraid, as if you were a small child, to show *this* anger. It is tragic that your mother can't help you now to do the work that only you can do. But it might be a good, relieving feeling for you to know that she could help *herself* and that you are free to eventually help the small child you once were to stay true to himself. You don't need to forgive to feel free (anyway, it would not work); you need the free access to your true feelings (without moralistic and religious prescriptions). The obligation to forgive (for what reason and for whose benefit?) conceals this access.

7 ⊕ Denial in Psychoanalytic Circles

I can feel with you because the same thing happened to me, too, but I never regretted staying true to my knowledge. And—like you—I learned from these experiences how denial works, how the fear of losing the acceptance of the group (the mother?) brings "intelligent" people to support nonsense so that they will not be abandoned. I learned recently that both Kohut and Ferenczi died from blood cancer, an illness that seems to be very rare. Both of them tried until the end to remain psychoanalysts and to be recognized as such, although what they found out was clearly opposed to Freud. They found the suffering of the child that was not given mirroring, empathy, or understanding. However, they did not find the courage to see that psychoanalysis denies this reality or to clearly separate themselves from it. Both suffered a lot from their isolation within the analytical community and Ferenczi also from the cruel rejection by Freud, whom he loved like a father.

10 ⊕ Fear of Death

I am not sure if I understand your question well. I think that because the shock told you the truth about your father, you don't need to be shocked again. Now you know that you don't need *this* father, even if the child thought all your life that you did. You needed a good, caring, honest father, but not this one, not a father who scared you to death. This knowledge is very powerful, and it will give you company should the fear of death come up again.

You will know why it came and from where, and that the danger was real in your past but not today.

12 ♾ *Psychosomatic Symptoms and Working Through the Pain III*

I read your frank, honest letter twice and was very moved by your desperate search for love and understanding from your family. You can't believe that they don't understand even your simple sentence: "Please look at me." They can't because their hearts are frozen. The advantage of your search is clear—you will be unable to deny this reality again. Even if by so strongly feeling your solitude you are in danger of betraying again the child you have been, your body will warn you at times, through corporal pain, should you again become a victim of self-betrayal. A child can't live without the illusion of loving parents; the adult can if he wants to. He may want to because he already knows the terrible price he would have to pay for a new illusion.

12 ♾ *An Incredible Pain*

You write: "I really hope one day I will be able to express my full and real self, not all the masks I had to wear in search of acceptance all my life." Why should you not be able to do that? Keep in mind that you don't owe anybody fake feelings; that you are as free as anybody to feel the rage without feeling guilty, because every emotion has its causes and you must not minimize them. As adults, we *can* live without our parents' love, only as children we needed it to survive. I think that your pain is the result of forcing yourself to feel what you *think* you should feel. Your body doesn't want this; it needs your emotional honesty.

12 ৬ *Karma?*

Preaching that abusers are teachers and that you can make sense of the endured abuse by turning negative energies into positive ones is a very problematic philosophy. It is used for brainwashing everywhere. In this way "teachers" pass on to others the lies that they were told and that caused their rage so they can feel well and "positive."

14 ৬ *The Fear After Childbirth*

Maybe the book *The Truth Will Set You Free* will be helpful, but above all try to *feel* your emotions, to take them seriously and talk about them to your partner or friends. They want to tell you something you need to know. Don't take antidepressants.

15 ৬ *An Incredible Pain*

Your thoughtful letter reminded me of another one written here in German and saying: "I'd rather be healthy without parents than sick with them. (The famous French writer Marcel Proust, who died very early, wrote to his mother: I prefer to have my illness and be loved by you rather than to be in good shape but lose your love). You are so right when you write that animals don't need to exploit their children or their lives; they let them go and give them their liberty. It is only the human being that burdens the children with lifelong feelings of guilt. I congratulate you on your insight and hope it will help you to resist every kind of blackmail.

16 ⌖ *The Bad Genes?*

Does your solidarity mean that you no longer believe in the fairy tale of bad genes? Dropping this "theory" may lessen the number of your fans, but it gives you a solid basis for serious research and opens your eyes to the real sources of violence that are always hidden in cruel child upbringing that I call child mistreatment. These were the causes of Hitler's rise. If we believe that people are born with bad genes, we would have to say that many millions of bad babies were born in Germany around thirty years before the Third Reich and they became willing executors of Hitler's perverse orders. Have you also read my latest book, *The Body Never Lies?*

18 ⌖ *No "Evil Genes"*

We publish your letter for people who do not yet fully understand how the dynamic of child abuse works and how the myth of the bad child serves to excuse the abuse of one's own children. People who understand this dynamic don't need any "scientific" proofs of this kind. They know that neither mental illness nor extreme cruelty come from bad genes, and they know *why*.

20 ⌖ *My Story*

I am glad that you feel freer after you decided to face your terrible truth. You have much courage, and I am sure that once you have done this work you will feel much better—provided that your therapists have also the courage you have and will not try to feed you with illusions and moralistic "consolations."

20 ⌖ *Diagnonsense*

I think that these are not exceptions and that many illnesses are *produced* by diagnoses which conceal the true causes of the symptom and are treated with drugs that produce new symptoms. It is good that you write and publish your letters wherever you can do it.

21 ⌖ *Why Can't You Recommend a Therapist?*

If I knew of some therapists who would be respectful enough to answer your questions; free enough to show indignation about what your parents have done to you; empathic enough when you need to release your pent-up rage; wise enough not to preach forgetting, forgiveness, meditation, positive thinking; honest enough not to offer you empty words like "spirituality," when they feel scared by your history, I would be happy to give you their names, addresses, and phone numbers. Unfortunately, I don't know them, but I still like to hope that they exist. However, when I am looking for them on the Internet, I find plenty of esoteric and religious offers, plenty of denial, commercial interests, and traditional traps, but not at all what I am looking for. For that reason I give you my FAQ list for your own research. If a therapist refuses to answer your questions right from the start, you can be sure that by leaving him you can save yourself time and money. If you don't dare to ask questions out of fear of your parents, your fear may be highly understandable.

However, trying to do it anyway may be useful because your questions are important and by daring to ask them you can only win.

22 ~ *Psychiatry and Abuse*

Your case story is very interesting. You see how the patient regained her trust in her own memory when you didn't refuse to believe her like the other doctor did. But I think that believing in a neutral position is not enough. The patient needed more; she needed your *indignation* about the deeds of her perpetrators. Most doctors don't dare to feel and to show this feeling because they pity their own parents and are afraid to lose their love if they are appalled about parents' cruelty. Can you remember how you reacted to the story of abuse in this case?

22 ~ *Your Decision*

It is almost unbearable for a child not to be seen, not to be listened to; he must deny this knowledge. Most people continue it for their whole lives. But you decided to feel the pain, and now nobody can hurt you in this way again because *you* listen to yourself.

23 ~ *An Incredible Pain*

To heal a broken bone you don't need to break it again. You don't need a dangerous regressive therapy to learn to feel, because you *can* feel the rage; it is stored up in your body, but it will not leave you until you are willing to understand its cause. Nobody has feelings without reasons. It is not about parents' "mistakes," it is about their probably very scary behavior toward the child you once were.

It can be this fear that hinders you in seeing the causes of your rage and makes you feel guilty instead. Your last letter was very insightful; try to stay true to yourself and don't allow anybody to confuse you. A father can't be the enlightened witness or therapist to his son who suffered from him as a child. This would be highly confusing. You write, "I don't know if this is the right thing to do. I don't think so." Trust your feelings; they know what happened to you, and they will guide you.

23 ♈ *Unbelievable*

Your story reminds me of my own experiences with my Freudian colleagues. They always followed the rule that we should not believe what the patients tried to remember, and the patients accepted this willingly because they wanted to avoid the pain of the truth and thus hoped that their memories were only fantasies, made-up stories. When I insisted on the reality of these memories, my colleagues became irritated, all of them.

24 ♈ *I Feel Imprisoned by My Past*

You write: "His father was the perpetrator. But the boy wanted no one but his father. That is how I feel. No matter what my parents have done, I needed them, and sometimes feel that I still do." The story about the father and his son shows that you know exactly what you need: to rebel against your parents instead of waiting for them to change. I think that you are able to take this step, but it is possible that the medication you have been taking for years makes it difficult for you. Can you now, when you have a good partner, good friends, and a job you like, try to live without any medication? The pain may increase for a while, but if you really want to liberate yourself from your past, you must stop waiting for the love of people who never loved you, who are just unable to love. As a child, you needed your parents as the boy in your story, but now *you don't need abusive parents*: open your eyes and don't let any medication keep them closed.

25 & Hormonal Imbalance Due to Fear?

To me there is no doubt that children who have lived with fear and unpredictability develop a cortical imbalance. Children who are spanked in the first years of their lives develop *many* kinds of imbalances, and usually doctors try to counteract this imbalance with drugs that are harmful. Even if the parents of grown-up children could change and become loving, this would not alter the malfunctioning of the body because the symptoms (like arthritis) imprison the never-expressed rage of the once-mistreated child. Only by experiencing these emotions and understanding the justified rage can we get away from the terrible pain. Medication "helps" only for a while and usually hinders the appearance of feelings and the development of understanding.

25 & Help for Pedophiles

You write: "I was also sexually abused as a child. I did not become a pedophile, but I did suffer a lot with the idea that I liked and attracted the abuse. I was able to get over sexual abuse after I put the blame on my abusers." So you know quite well what your friend has to do. But if he protects his abusers and doesn't want to suffer, doesn't want to *feel* his truth, nobody can force him. It does not have to take fourteen years if one finds a good therapist.

25 ⌘ *Terrifying Nightmares of Children*

Nobody wants to believe that their horrible memories and dreams are real histories, especially when the parents deny everything. If I remember well, your mother said "Shame on you" when you wanted to talk with her about your father's abuse. Such a mother is able to confuse her child completely and to burden her with terrible feelings of guilt at a very tender age. Your dream shows you what she *always* has done. It opens your eyes. You are thus no longer in real danger, as long as you don't try to protect her again. The danger today is your illusion: that she will read and understand your novels, that she will show empathy and will stay on your side. She has clearly showed that she will not. The dream tells you the truth that you would prefer not to know, but it is certainly more healing to know it than to deny it.

29 ⌘ *The Trap of Pretense*

I am happy that you no longer cling to the illusion you so clearly describe: that the abusive mother totally changed. I agree with everything you are saying here. You really got it. For the new edition of *Paths of Life*, I wrote a postscript that confirms exactly how right you are in what you are writing

SEPTEMBER 2007

1 ℰ Betraying Your Needs

You seem to see exactly how your parents treated you, and what you had to do to save your health was to see particularly how you betrayed your needs by helping these parents because you thought it humane to participate in the settlement of their care. I think that you are right in calling this a mistake. It is very hard to give up the illusion of eventually having loving parents who will be grateful for having such a good daughter, even when she was treated sadistically. But your body doesn't agree with your hopes, because it knows your parents better than your mind and it wants to protect you. Listen to your body; being a slave is in your past. Today you are free to make a change and say no to people who were so cruel to you. Where is your rage?

3 ℰ Creating Humanity

I think that you have always wanted to be good and human, and to decrease or even undo the pain your siblings had to suffer— to create humanity where your parents created horror. This may have given you the strength to survive with self-respect; it was the source of your self-esteem. But the very small girl also had to suffer terribly, and nobody was there to hold her and to tell her: They are sadistic with you, too; they don't deserve your love, your compassion, and your understanding. All this is poisoning your body, and it hinders your true compassion for the small girl who always had to be tough and help others without any complaints. It is time for her rebellion.

4 ᘓ I Can Finally Listen to Myself, Can Feel, Think, and Speak Up

I can hardly believe that this letter was written by the same person who waited a few months ago for their mother to read writings, appreciate their contents, and finally fathom what she did to you. Instead of doing that, she said, "Shame on you." You seem to have grown up so quickly because you allow yourself to feel and to understand your rage. Should it turn out that your therapist is unable to grow at the same speed, you don't have to wait for him to do so. It is your life and your freedom to talk that you can now enjoy, and I think that nobody's limits can stop you from using your eyes, your brain, and your heart the way they need to be used. You are so right about rejecting confusing theories, and your arguments are absolutely convincing to me.

6 ᘓ I Finally Listen to Myself

With this letter you might eventually reach the small, unprotected girl. Stay with her; don't abandon her anymore. She needs you, your love and your protection—nothing more.

7 ᘓ Abuse Is Never Love

I have the impression that the notion of a "harmful love" still conceals and disguises the simple but very painful and scary fact of abuse. I see the betrayal on the side of the abuser and the illusion of love on the side of the child. To me, real love is never harmful, and abuse is never love. Concerning grandparents, I don't like to make general statements; if I don't know the specific family situation, I prefer not to make any judgments.

8 ⸙ Fear

You know everything that you need to know, but you are probably still very much afraid of feeling the rage toward your parents and of staying true to your feelings. Instead, you suffer from insomnia and physical pain that most likely remind you of being beaten in childhood. You write: "It was Father's day today and I called my Dad. I felt obligated. I said, 'Happy Father's Day,' and I wanted to vomit. I actually 'gave him the finger' through the phone as I was talking to him. But part of me just 'had' to call him. I know as long as I do this that I am not sympathizing with the child that I once was. I am forgiving my father (ditto for my mom), and they do not deserve it. As long as I continue to do this, I choose them—I forgive them and respect them, more than me. I'm saying what they did to me and the way they treated me is okay, and it's not. It's just not." There is nothing I have to add to your words except to tell you that the fear, which stops you from doing what you feel would be the right thing for you, is the fear of a very small boy who must have been in mortal danger if he tried to defend himself. Today this danger is not real. Try to explain this to the scared child who has been living in your body for forty years and who still believes that his mother is "a saint," even when you as a grown-up see her coldness and indifference. Try to talk to this child; he will have much to tell you—things that you never dreamt of before. You are on the best path to liberate yourself from your fear, which is fully understandable when you take into account the terror of your childhood.

8 ⸵ *Emotional Abuse of My Stepson*

I am very sorry that I can't give you any advice. I can only say that if I were in this tragic situation and had to see how this woman destroys the love of a child I loved, I would do everything I could to make her access to him impossible. How you can obtain such a solution where you live, I don't know. In any event, it is a crime to use the child in her battle against you, and he is absolutely put under constant stress between two mothers; he shows his fear very clearly.

12 ⸵ *Lost Again*

Denial is the main defense of an alcoholic. It is thus no wonder that you "learned" it from your father. But he didn't know what he was doing, and you do. You have the courage to question your behavior and to look for its sources. I have no doubt that you will overcome this state, that you will feel the plight of the little boy, the victim of your father's denial, and he will feel increasingly safe with you. He will not need to behave like your father did.

18 ⸵ *I Hate Them—I'm Similar to Them— I Love Me?!*

No, you are not with your children like your parents were with you. Far from that. If you repeat something, you do it to protect your parents from your rage so that you can avoid seeing how mean your parents were. After your mother refused to come to your child, you went to play golf so that you could say: The way my mother behaves is quite normal—it is normal to ignore a kid; I do it too.

It is normal to have a hole instead of a heart. But you *do have* a heart; you only need the courage to look at your parents and to feel the rage. People who were most tortured in childhood are very reluctant to see their truth and to feel their rage because they are afraid of being punished again. Out of this fear they pretend that "it was not so bad." But now you cannot be punished and will not be hurt again—unless you again have the idea to ask your mother for a favor. Soon you will learn to protect yourself and ask other people for help. There are a lot of people out there who will not hurt you when you need them.

18 ᘓ *Children*

They don't damage the bones of small children in America and Britain like they do in Iraq; at least they don't do it to so many. But they damage them, most of them, by spanking them and causing lesions in their brains. In this way a new generation of ignorant people is being produced, people who mistreat their children and pretend to do this for their own good.

24 ᘓ *Facts and Pessimism*

We seem to agree about the issue of therapy: that working on one's own history is a way to heal the effects of child abuse and its denial. But there is still another question that bothers us and seems not to bother you, namely: Why is this knowledge (for us so easy to understand) globally denied, ignored, feared, and avoided? What causes this ignorance and blindness of abusers, cruel parents, doctors, lawyers, and why don't they understand the simplest connections? In our opinion they are hindered by the lesions in their mind, caused by the fear learned as a tormented baby and toddler. Why can only a few people realize that spanking children produces a violent and sick society? How do you answer to this question? Please, answer *only* this one.

27 ❧ *All Child Abuse Causes Brain Damage*

It was your courage to see your own parents that gave you the capacity to understand more than some scientists can, because they never got in touch with their feelings. They write about irreversible brain damage without having knowledge of successful therapies. In fact, the majority of the population absolutely confirms their beliefs that the damage caused by child abuse can't be cured if they refuse to work on it in therapy. On the other hand, we can see in this mailbox that there are people who overcame their fear and got rid of their symptoms by daring to see what their parents had done to them and to rebel against cruelty and injustices endured in their childhood.

29 ❧ *Eventually, the Anger*

You write: "Now I validate my own anger. I work for sympathy for myself from myself. I realize whenever I feel a 'mean' feeling toward a child, that this is the abusive 'parent's' feeling that was directed at me when I was a child. I imagine how it felt to have been the recipient of that mean feeling. How it broke my heart. The 'mean' feeling diminishes." There is nothing I can add. You are on the right path to changing your life and to rescuing your son, and I am sure that you will succeed, because you have the courage to see and feel the *causes* of your plight. You were never a bad person; you were only misled by your therapists, who didn't allow you to respect your true feelings.

29 ⌇ Migraines and Fibromyalgia

You write: "Although I feel better each day and I'm out of the hole I was in, I do still have to battle physical pain. In the past year my body pains from fibromyalgia and migraines have greatly lessened, but they have not gone away." Why don't you trust that your body can do more if you stay on the right path you have dared to find? The pains may tell you that there is still more past cruelty that you will have to face. You need time to do this. One year might be not enough to fathom what you had to suffer over so many years, but I don't doubt that you will succeed to live without corporal pain once you fully give up the denial. Be patient; it takes time— sometimes much time. Fibromyalgia is a very cruel illness, as cruel as your parents' emotional brutality that you may be afraid to see and feel.

29 ⌇ Colic and Hurtful Parenting

Yes, of course, colic is a name for the child's reaction to the lack of love and the refusal of communication, to cruel behavior of parents who talk about "colics" instead of taking their child in their arms and soothing his or her pain. It is good for you and for your child that you can understand that.

30 ❦ *Biomedical Scientists Score Higher in Autism-Spectrum Traits*

Your letter explains very clearly why the discoveries of brain researchers have not been used to better understand the plight of the human being who experienced fear early in life. To understand these connections we need to be in touch with our own emotions. If we are disconnected from them, we lack empathy for ourselves and for others, and our "discoveries" made with the help of computers may remain fruitless even though they are spectacular and could save millions of lives by reducing the global ignorance of spankers. Your links explain why most people to this day (including scientists) still don't realize that child abuse and the denial of its danger are nothing less than the effect of endured child abuse that left behind damage in the brain of the once-spanked abusers.

OCTOBER 2007

6 ❦ *Colic*

What you write makes much sense; you don't need to worry if the relationship turned out to be good. It is also possible that her birth reawakened some sad memories in you from *your* birth, but you succeeded in overcoming them after she was three months old.

7 ❦ *An Incredible Pain*

I realize now that my answer to you didn't come through and am sorry about this. I wrote to you that it is very painful to feel that you were not loved, not seen, not understood, and were so alone with this pain. To show you that many well-known people suffered the same destiny, I sent you a quote from the famous composer Igor Stravinsky. You can find this quote in my book *The Drama of the Gifted Child*, p. 38, footnote. I wrote also to you that the pain of your childhood must have been so strong that you were forced to repress it, but your body kept it, so you can eventually fully feel it as an adult and, in time, get rid of it. Consciously felt pain doesn't last forever. Once you know it, it will leave you and make you free for other emotions because you will no longer need your energies for suppressing your truth. And you will become stronger, because you will not be afraid of painful memories coming up. They will acquire a context and be no longer so scary.

11 ⟡ Aftermath

Yes, you do have solid reasons for a better future. Once you gave up your illusion of eventually getting the love of your parents, you became free. It was the fear of being punished for the truth and the misleading "philosophy" of your therapists that blocked your progress and increased your fear. Fortunately, you could overcome this fear and allow yourself to see and feel your truth.

12 ⟡ Wonderful Research and Texts

I am glad that you found a therapist who helps you to see and bear your truth. Everything falls into place then, doesn't it?

13 ❧ Dangerous Parents

Why do you want me to believe in psychoanalytical constructions that I have criticized for more than the last twenty-five years? Your first letter was so confused that I could not understand your question, nor could you understand mine. But now I feel that you can understand me. The real parents of the child *were* dangerous, but as adults we can learn to free ourselves from our dependency on those parents so that they no longer have any power over us. The analytical construction of dangerous internal parents only proves that analytical therapists still live in a state of fear as long as they deny the cruelty of their *real* parents. Unfortunately, most of them deny this fact, accuse the child (above all Melanie Klein and her followers like Otto Kernberg and others) and thus make it impossible for their patients to recognize the torture they were submitted to in childhood. Their patients also stay caught within these fears for decades. Why do you go to psychoanalysts?

14 ❧ Long Journey Indeed

After having taken antidepressants for a long time, it is quite normal that you can't free yourself as quickly as you want to. But you are on the path to doing so because you now understand how healing works. The biggest obstacles that you might have to combat are the voices you quote: "Oh, come on, grow up, get a life, stop playing the victim, you are just unable, unfit, stop hiding behind this unhappy-childhood sob story, so many people have had it much harder, you have always been this impossible person, take your medicine and stop pitying yourself, etc." You need perhaps to look in the eyes of the persons who talked to you this way (or are still doing so?) and realize how destructive their behavior is. Do you need to listen to them now? Have you read the article on depression on my Web site?

15 ◌ *An Open Letter of Gratitude*

I can understand your indignation about the hypocrisy of governments that "care" about children, and I share your feelings. But I have no solution to suggest to you. What you are doing is still the best: to question absurd statements, to show these people the absurdity of their arguments. But most of them are not accessible to your questions because their logic is based on their fear of their parents and on the messages they got from them when they were three to four years old—that children need to be spanked. These messages seem to be stronger than what we say or write. They seem to be the hard disk in people's brain computers. However, we must continue to talk and to write, as you rightly do.

15 ◌ *A Letter from the Invisible Man*

I am glad that you eventually decided to leave the hiding place and come out in the open air. As you see, your philosophy was not able to fully protect you from the dangers of your family. Now you seem to realize that the dangers you tried to avoid were actually real, but that today your mother can no longer hurt you unless you continue to allow her to do so.

15 & Not Giving Up

You didn't give up and now you found the small girl playing in the sand. You will learn a lot from her, I am sure. Good luck to both of you!

15 & Nightmares and Novels of Horror

Why do you need to look for more memories? You know enough to understand what happened to you, and I know it from you. But I think that you can't believe that all this cruelty really happened, that your mother told you "Shame on you" when you tried to tell her what your father did to you and you needed her help. This reaction from a mother is so horrible that I can understand that you hesitate to believe. So you want to find more details, to convince me, your therapist, and maybe others about your right to be enraged. Actually, you want to convince yourself to believe eventually that the horror was indeed real. With a mother who denied everything and made you feel guilty, you are afraid of feeling your rage, but it is this rage that will help you to leave your family alone and become true to yourself. Does your therapist prevent you from feeling this rage? Can it be that he is afraid of it and you want to protect him?

20 & Thanks from a Replacement Child

I am glad that you found the story of van Gogh. No matter what he could provide, it was never enough for his mother because the other Vincent was the one she "loved." Would she have loved him also if he had not been dead? You *are* on the right path and fortunately your body helped you to recognize the confusion of your therapist and decide to stop seeing him. Now you no longer can be fooled.

21 ⌘ Thank You and Info Request

I think that if you want to help children you need to work with parents on *their histories*, to help them to find out what stops them from being the parents their children need in order to feel protected, respected, and loved. To do this, work with a clear knowledge of your own history could help you more than a university degree.

26 ⌘ To Protect Your Child

I am so happy that my book could support your feelings and help you to stay true to them. Of course, you should not go back to your abusive parents; your childhood was a hell. Now they want to destroy your well-being with your family, to make you unhappy and dependent on them again, and they want to continue their destructive work by exploiting your child. Fortunately, you have the insight, the courage, and the strength to protect yourself and your family from them.

28 ⌘ I Don't Want to Give Up!

You write: "So my question then is, is there some way to self-validate when one is isolated, some way to lead oneself through the mourning and recovery process so that one can choose to live rather than to give up?" In my opinion you made it clear that you understand enough to not want to destroy your memory and thereby give up. You know your history and are on the best path to becoming free of its effects. *Don't* give up—you *do* have a choice. Making the right choice will give you the self-validation you are looking for.

28 ⌖ *Using Medication*

You write: "I am seeking your opinion about my continued use of these drugs. Will they prevent me from being able to access these repressed feelings? I am afraid that if I stop taking them, I will be unable to work. I am also afraid of withdrawal from these unfortunately very addictive medications. Any advice you could provide would be appreciated." I can't change your reality. If you think you can only work when you take the medication even though you see the danger of losing your true self, I am unable to give you any advice. It is up to you to make the choice. You are well informed about the effects of your medication and I can only say that in my opinion you will not lose the capacity to work if you decide to live with your true self. I think that the opposite is true. But it is possible that you will have to change the "work" you are doing now.

30 ⌖ *Do I Need to Know More?*

You write: "Something traumatic must have happened at that time, but I cannot recall it." What are you looking for if you already know this: "My mother had never wanted a child and made that quite clear to me; she told me so. She tried to abandon me many times. She deliberately made it her mission in life to ruin mine. After all, she reasoned, I had ruined her life by being born; fair is fair.

She was a closet lesbian and sexually abused me." What you need is to *feel* the suffering of this small girl who was not wanted, was frequently in danger of becoming abandoned, and was sexually abused. This knowledge is sufficient to make you very angry with your mother and become the loving mother of this tortured little girl who is still in search of a caring, empathic mother.

NOVEMBER 2007

2 ℰ *Finally!*

You write: "They stole my anger and I want to get it back." You *can* get it back, and it will help you to heal. It will give you the courage to own your true feelings and never allow anybody to steal them. You need them more than anything else.

9 ℰ *She Eats Me*

She could try to eat your child, but she can't eat your adult self unless you allow her to do so. You must protect yourself clearly by defending your limits and saying no.

11 ℰ *Follow-Up*

So I wasn't far away from the truth; I had the right intuition when I wrote that you know how healing works. You will have times like you describe here, and also dark times when old memories will dare to come up, but you will no longer forget or abandon yourself. The wonderful dream shows it very clearly.

23 &c *The Danger of AA*

I have written many times about the dangers of AA, of this kind of manipulation, hypocrisy, poisonous pedagogy, and confusion. You see that you felt the negative influence of this "treatment" when you write, "I went into this meeting, but such rage rose in me that I had to leave." Your rage is understandable, and if your therapist regards it as harmless, he may no longer be the right therapist for you.

25 &c *A Letter to My Father*

I was distressed to the core when I read your letter, for which I thank you wholeheartedly. At the same time, I felt a sort of gratefulness for the fate that helped the lively, brave, and bright little girl not only to survive the terrible jail of her horrific parents but also to keep the full clarity and courage needed to see and to accuse, without "buts," without illusions, without self-betrayal. This stance is very rarely encountered, and your letter will certainly help others to recognize their own situation and to forgo the buts. If you have no objections, we can also publish your letter in French. I would like to do this because here your child also has the strength to speak for countless other children who are forced to bear the more or less visible delusions of their parents for years and to experience that as normal. Formed by this ignorance, they often remain blind to the suffering of children their entire lives and still recommend physical punishment. They work in senseless "research" for the pharmaceutical industry, organize wars, produce cruel movies, and don't know at all that they still "live" in the prison of their sick parents because they never had the courage to see through their parents' delusions. Thus they continue to poison the world with the toxin that they had to swallow as children.

30 ❧ Nursing Homes

You have done well. Even if they pretend to be deaf, something may nevertheless bother them if they receive messages like yours often enough. We have no other choice than to write and to hope that one day the truth will be heard. Words can be stronger than arms, which show fear rather than strength.

30 ❧ A Note of Gratitude

Your letter is full of determination, consciousness, and clarity. It is impossible to overcome the aggressions of your father and the lies of your mother, or both, without a lot of rage that you had to repress over such a long time at the cost of your body. Fortunately, you can feel and understand this rage now thanks to the empathy of your counselor, so you are becoming more and more free to live your authentic feelings.

DECEMBER 2007
2 ❧ The Journey Home to Our True Self

You write: "I had been terrorized to feel I must love my mother! I realized that a part of me was trying to love her and that I did not feel love for her. I only felt fear my entire life, fear of my mother, not love. When I let this go from my body, this attempt to force the feeling of love, a major shift happened. Since that time, my days are free from this undercurrent of anxiety." With these few words you describe a situation that millions of people probably share with you without having the courage to voice it. I am so glad that you could eventually feel this pressure and reject it, and that you now can feel the liberation you can find when you decide to be true to your real feelings without lying to yourself. All religions, however, demand the opposite from us. How can so many people believe in a God that wants us to lie to ourselves and call these lies a *virtue*?

2 ❧ Detachment from Parents

It is correct and logical that, if you didn't have good parental attachment as a child, you will look for it your whole life in the hope that you will get what you so painfully missed when you needed it most. You can't easily detach yourself and are waiting for your parents to change, unless you realize in your therapy how much you suffered because of your lack of attachment and take steps to overcome this loss. Waiting for them to change will only increase your dependency on your parents, because usually they don't change. And even if they do, you still need to feel and understand the pain of the small, abandoned, and hurt child you once were so that you can understand and resolve your plight of today. As an adult, you don't need abusive parents, not at all. Unfortunately, in childhood there was no other choice.

2 ❧ The Importance of Finding One Empathic Person

Your letter shows how much we can change even in the most tragic situations if even one person (your teacher?) is clearly, without any buts and pedagogy, on the side of the mistreated child. Unfortunately, this attitude is very rare. None of our presidents, religious leaders, popes, and other people in power, none of the philosophers, well-known authors, filmmakers, and actors, seem to see that children all around are being mistreated, tortured, daily, every minute. This fact means our activity is needed to save their lives, and also to save our future from criminals and mad dictators.

7 ❧ Enlightened Witness Revisited by Science

You are asking what we think about the article you sent us. I personally feel that it is better to admit 10 percent of the truth than nothing, but I prefer of course that one admits 100 percent (and definitely with fewer words than it has been done here). The lack of serotonin is not the cause of depression; it is one of the symptoms. And the cause is not genetic; it is the necessity of repressing strong genuine emotions like rage and sadness in an abusive family. And the "social support" will not work as long as there is so much fear about acknowledging the devastating role of abusive parents who teach their children from the beginning of their lives to suppress their vital emotions—not to cry, not to scream, to learn obedience, etc. An enlightened witness, in contrast, is a person who can listen to the victim with indignation, without being scared by her story.

16 ❧ We're Not Doomed to Repeat

No, we are only doomed to repeat what happened to us as long as we deny it. If we have the courage to know the truth of our childhood, if we don't need the lies to protect our parents, we *can* change. Unfortunately, our whole society and *all* religions prefer to protect the parents and let the child suffer by calling beatings "education." You can find the list of my thirteen books on my Web site.

16 ☙ The Facts Denied

Your honest and moving letter will strongly resonate with most of our readers. I don't doubt that every illness children (and adults) have to suffer is linked to the physical and emotional mistreatment and neglect they endured in their childhood. Unfortunately, this link is strongly denied by doctors, and indeed whole society.

18 ☙ Separation from the Soul

Yes, you are right; the price of being comatose is the heartbreaking separation of the soul. For that reason, people who did overcome this separation rarely find understanding in their families. They often feel as if they are talking to a wall. Separation from the soul happens so frequently that it seems to be the normal state. Thus cruelty and even sadism against children can go on and on without the slightest memory of the once-endured pain.

18 ☙ Pea Soup

You will not find anything other than what you have already stored in your body without knowing it. Knowing it can only help.

19 ⌀ *Thank You!*

I like to know that looking at your bookshelves and seeing my book helps you not to spank your child.

22 ⌀ *Santa Claus and Deception*

Since you have read the first chapter of *Banished Knowledge*, you may know what I think about this kind of child abuse. It is a way of fooling children into submission and blinding them to realities.

23 ⌀ *The Truth Is Not (Say Not)*
a Punishable Offense

You are absolutely right; the truth is not an offense, but we were punished for seeing it so many times. You are lucky that you can remember this incident well, so you can work on this memory. Millions of children suffered the same treatment, but they can't recall it and have never gained the insight you have. Your letter may help others to recall similar situations.

25 ⌀ *What Should I Do?*

Continue listening to your feelings and trying to understand what they are telling you. You seem to have had good experiences with that. Why should you abandon yourself again for new illusions?

26 ⁊ Problems with the Word "Discipline"

I very much agree with you concerning the word "discipline." I never use it. I also became skeptical toward authors who do use it, and I no longer recommend them.

26 ⁊ I Believe in Santa Again

You got it! Your letter shows that a book can help one to understand oneself and to begin to love oneself. By understanding that you can't love anybody whom you fear, you have already made a big progress that will save the rest of your life. This discovery will help you to avoid much unnecessary suffering—futile attempts to love and to elicit love where this is impossible and self-destructive. I needed many more years to understand that. And as you see on my Web site, so many people try and try to succeed in respecting a law that is based on a lie.

28 ⁊ Avoiding the Truth

Open the "Flyers" page on my Web site and read the text "21 Points." In my opinion, memories are always true, even if not exact, but the idea that traumas can be invented is one of the most serious psychoanalytical errors, because we don't need the memory of our suffering to survive; as children, we needed the repression. Therefore we *may* invent stories, but they will always be less harmful than the real trauma itself. The answer of your therapist seems to be avoiding the main issue.

29 ⚭ Hatred and Pain

In your heartbreaking letter, you say that mornings are better after you cry at night and that you have learned to respect and understand your feelings so that you will no longer hate yourself. You don't deserve to be hated; once you can fully hate the people who made you suffer so much, the pain will go away, you will breathe freely, and you will feel free.

31 ⚭ How Long Will It Take?

I think that you will suffer as long as the little girl in you is waiting for your father to understand your torture, to take a risk, to love you and to save you instead of protecting himself. But once you can rebel against him, the small girl will feel protected. Does this make sense to you? Try to see and feel how he betrayed you through his cowardice.

IV

FROM JANUARY TO JULY

2008

JANUARY 2008

5 ⤳ *Terror and Panic*

Yes, you are right, the illusion made you ill. But now you seem to be very close to your truth, and I am thus very hopeful that you will succeed in getting what you so much wanted: to know your true feelings and needs and to live your own life. It takes time, of course, but your tears show that you are on your path.

5 ⤳ *The Spiritual Ideology of "Negative Emotions"*

Your thoughtful letter is so clear and true, and I think that it could help many people to understand important connections. If you want to have it published on our Web site, please let us know, and we will do this with pleasure.

Thank you for your permission to publish your earlier letter, which I loved. I can't understand why you think that you have Asperger's syndrome. To me you are absolutely far away from it because you are a feeling person; otherwise you wouldn't have been able to write the letters you have written.

7 ❧ Reader's Question Regarding Emotional Memory

You are certainly right to look for the keys in your actual feelings—in this case guilt. There are mothers who scream at a baby, often shaking him and holding his arms when blaming him of being nasty. Why nasty? Just because he cried? Perhaps he felt uncomfortable. Instead of looking for the actual reason for his crying, they punish him. Does it make sense to you that your body tries to tell you a story like that using your forearms? I can't know it for sure, since you did not tell us at all how your mother "cared" for you.

16 ❧ Taking Things on Faith?

Thank you for saying that I don't need to be taken on faith. It is important to me that everybody can check what I am writing with the help of his or her own history.

18 ❧ The Reason for Child Abuse

Unfortunately, I can't promise you anything at the moment, but if you want to send me your book anyway, you can do it through my publishers in New York: Norton or Basic Books. As you read my books and are empathic with small children, I hope that you might be interested in my message that the sole reason for child abuse is the denial of the pain endured in our childhood. As almost everybody was beaten very early on, the denial of suffering became a part of our brain structure. My therapy concept is based on this fact, and it turns out that it helps survivors of mistreatments to liberate themselves from chronic symptoms if they want to know the truth about their childhood. I would be happy if you could make your patients and students aware of these facts by using the material published on my Web site (interviews, flyers, articles, and the mail).

19 ๛ Guilt

Freeing ourselves from the feelings of guilt imposed on us by others and never questioned by us already makes a big difference on our path to freedom.

20 ๛ Tantrum

A tantrum shows a deep despair and helplessness that a child is not able to express with words. An empathic adult will try to remember what happened right before it in order to understand what drove this child into despair and to let him know about it with empathy. That can help the child to understand himself. But never should a child be punished for his despair. Such stupid, cruel advice shows why children cannot express themselves other than through a tantrum. Let us assume that your friend is coming to you and is sobbing without being able to tell you why. Would you lock her up in a room as punishment to make her stop? Such advice is given to parents when children are at stake.

21 ๛ Two Years Later

Your letter is strong and true; it will encourage others to take their feelings seriously and not force themselves to believe in lies in order to save illusions. Hence it is exactly because of our illusions that we become sick. You saved your life, your future.

31 ᘓ *My Therapist Is Violent and a Liar*

A person who scares you can never help you, and if she lies, she is also dangerous. Why don't you leave her immediately? You seem to know exactly what you have to do. Why are you hesitating? Is it because you had to learn very early on to live with such a danger and to tolerate it? Today you are free to refuse this. Look for another therapist or read more on my Web site. Above all, read my interviews and the FAQ list.

31 ᘓ *A Letter from Greece*

To travel for two hours to Athens to be received by somebody who doesn't talk to you, who lets you talk for twenty minutes instead of an hour as was agreed upon, is totally absurd. You are tolerating this extreme abuse like a small helpless child who has no other options. But now, as an adult, you are not forced to endure this arrogance. As you so strongly reacted to *The Drama*, you are able to help yourself. Try to read my interviews on my Web site and my other books, especially *The Body Never Lies*, which is already available in Greek (if I am informed correctly). This book may awaken more feelings in you. Try to find in your town a person with a heart who can listen to you. You can also try to write letters to the small boy you once were, who never had a helping witness. You can become his witness. But traveling to Athens to be humiliated by this person who calls himself a therapist doesn't make sense at all, unless you go once—but only once!—to tell him how you feel about his arrogance. *That* could help you indeed.

FEBRUARY 2008

1 ❧ *The Illness and Death of My Father*

You can only start from the place where you actually *are*, not where you *think* you should be. You are looking for the emotions of the small child that was abandoned by the father, when nobody gave you any information, nobody saw your suffering. Can you *feel* your suffering now about being not *seen*?

4 ❧ *Ending the Relationship with the Parents*

This is your *right* answer: "However, this time I am very determined to have my life back, discover my true identity, and pursue my own happiness." You must take it seriously; your body needs your determination. It will not wait until your parents understand. If they could, then everything would have happened differently. Nobody can force you to answer calls that you don't want to, since you are no longer a child.

5 ❧ *The Truth Is a Matter of Choice*

Yes, you made the choice and I want to congratulate you on your insight that the truth is a matter of choice. We are unable to convince anybody who doesn't want to know. S/he will take the newspaper and avoid listening to us. But we *can* find the courage to take seriously what we are seeing, feel the pain and no longer hope in vain that someday this person will understand. How could she if she doesn't want to? You can never, ever force anybody to understand the pain of their child if they refuse to understand their own pain.

23 ⌁ A *Response to* The Body Never Lies

I have the feeling that you read my book with your eyes totally closed. How did you manage this? The answer to your question actually lies in the book: Society is composed of people so thoroughly terrorized in early childhood that they are, like you, even as adults, still too afraid to see what has been done to them by their own parents.

25 ⌁ *Dealing with Incomplete Memories*

Probably, your memories will become more and more clear once your fear of blaming your mother—and hence your need to protect her—lessens. Memories can come in dreams, and they can also show themselves in the way you feel when confronted with lies, pretensions, and abuse. Since you are now ready to see your past without illusions, the doors can open and will do so with time. But the access is always the present: the sorrow, the rage, the shame. The path from fear to courage may seem too long for the little boy, but now he will be protected by the adult he became and will thus succeed.

25 ⌁ *Chekhov and Corporal Punishment*

Chekhov could see the truth in all of his writings, especially in *Uncle Vanya,* but in his own life he was a most devoted son to his father. The strong fear of the severely beaten child did not allow him to protest.

26 ✑ Africa

It will be, as you say, a long way. But I am glad that you realized that violence is not the way to make children curious and eager to learn. Do you have any suggestions after this trip?

27 ✑ Learning from Children

I am really happy that you understand me so well and that you are able to learn so much from your child. You see how quickly children can be reached if we don't think that we must win a war with them.

MARCH 2008

3 ✑ Unwanted Children?

You are right: unwanted children are very often mistreated. However, there exist as a rule a huge number of people who were "wanted" indeed, but only for playing the role of the victims upon which their parents needed to be able to take revenge. They were wanted to give their parents what the parents had never received from *their* own parents: love, adoration, attention, and so many other things. Otherwise, why would so many people have five or more children when they have no time for them? Why do they adopt children if their body refuses to give them what they apparently "want?" The never acknowledged, never felt pain of their childhood calls for retribution. They go to church, they pray, they honor their parents, forgive them everything—and they mistreat their children at home, often in a very cruel way, as if this were the most natural thing, because they learned this so early. Their children also learn this perverted behavior very early, and will later do the same; and so this perverse behavior endures for millennia and will continue to do so unless people are willing to *see* the perversion of their parents and are ready to consciously refuse to imitate it. You are not being "sickeningly sarcastic"; you only dared to speak the truth that most people are afraid of seeing or talking about.

6 ℮ *Daring to Talk*

We publish your extremely moving letter because it will encourage others to leave their loneliness and to dare to talk about their suffering. I am so glad that you experienced how healing it can be to share your terrible story with a good friend. The cruel and mean answer given to you by your own mother might have discouraged you from talking for your whole life if you had not met your friend. Until then, the skin rash was the only language available to you. The way may be long, but there is no doubt that you will succeed in healing yourself because you have already had the experience of speaking the truth and winning.

7 ℮ *A Mother's Deep Concerns*

Have you already asked yourself why you left your son with his father and went far away to do your research despite what you knew about his father? It unfortunately happens very often that we unconsciously repeat what happened to us in our past if we never had the chance to work on our repressed emotions and the story of our childhood. We can have the best intentions, yet the repressed story hidden in our body lets us make decisions that we never would have wanted to make if we knew, emotionally knew, what happened to us when we were very small and at the mercy of our totally unconscious parents.

12 ❧ Nearly Insane

Your letter makes much sense and I congratulate you for the work you have done. You understand now that graduation in psychology means near to nothing if you are afraid of your truth, your emotions, and above all your justified rage.

16 ❧ How Do I Spread My New Knowledge?

People in authority will not help you; they need their authority above all and are afraid of the truth, of their own fear hidden behind that authority. But if you have time, you can print my flyers (they are free) and send them out to schools, to organizations pretending to help children, to nurses, to physicians—wherever you think that your information will get some interest, some curiosity, or even an open ear.

16 ❧ Is Obesity the Result of Childhood Abuse?

Yes, we can say this without any hesitation. Every behavior that is directed against the health of a person, that hinders the healthy functioning of the body and mind, is a repetition of once-endured mistreatment, neglect, confusion, lies, betrayal, perverted practices, and the exploitation of the child.

16 ⤫ *"Good Advice"*

Your letter shows how hopeless all these well-intended books are: the ones that tell the once-mistreated parents how they should behave toward their children without telling them that their violence, hate, and lack of love come from their own childhood and are blocking their best intentions. Even well-known books avoid this topic. They tell you how you can become a good mother, but they never mention how and when you learned to become cruel to your children. Obviously, in this way they protect your mother and father, and your children will have to pay for your tolerance toward your parents.

21 ⤫ *Strange Experience*

From where could the child learn to vent his anger if not his parents? The lesson was for a long time stored in his body because he was not allowed to show his anger; he didn't feel anything. Now, when you begin to feel, it makes sense that the anger first comes in the way that the child learned it from his father. But with time the adult will learn his *own* way of showing his feelings. Meanwhile, he must accept that *first* he reacts like his father or his mother. Fortunately, he can observe it, so he sees more and more how he was suffering in his childhood. Not many people have the courage to admit that they are imitating their parents; they don't want to be like them—ever. But acknowledging this can be beneficial.

APRIL 2008

9 ᕃ *Different Levels of Messages from the Body*

Yes, I want to encourage you to continue your journey to recovery. It makes sense that you can now better bear the pain (the truth), because we can't heal the wounds of our past by denying them or even laughing about them. We must learn to take them seriously.

19 ᕃ *A Year Later*

The fact that the rashes on your skin are disappearing shows that you are on the right path to yourself. Of course, you wanted your mother to validate your suffering, but you know now that this would never happen, even if she were still alive. However, now it is you who can and do validate your plight, and this is what you eventually need the most for your future.

20 ᕃ *Brooklyn Boy Reborn*

It took much time and much much suffering, I suppose, before you arrived where you are now. But eventually you have succeeded to understand yourself and no longer need to go back to Florida, where you spent two years fulfilling your guilt (what guilt?) and sense of obligation (what for?) to your mother. To not meet our torturers again seems necessary for our health.

26 &c *Why Psychoanalysis Isn't Effective*

Thank you for sharing your experience with us. Once I understood that psychoanalysis protects parents, it became clear to me that it can't help former victims to discover the reality of their childhoods and thus liberate themselves from the tragic effects.

27 &c *I No Longer Play Your Game*

I did read your letter and felt much moved by it. Congratulations on the courage and honesty that speak through your entire letter, especially where you write, "I have the biggest, biggest, biggest compulsions in this whole wide world to take care of her feelings, but her feelings are not my responsibility." *Exactly.* Only the former kid with his great smile is your responsibility. Don't abandon him, even if he has to cry for a while. Ask him if *he* needs to go to the funeral, and if he says no, respect what he is saying.

30 &c *Born into Heroin*

Your amazing letter is very strong and convincing; it shows that even a former child of heroin-addicted parents can help himself to heal if he dares to confront his truth, to feel and reject the lies and illusions suggested by society, religions, even by philosophy and therapies of all kind. I was very moved by your letter and also glad for you that you are not going to waste your time writing a philosophical thesis, thus avoiding the full truth about *your* story. Fortunately, you have dared to find it. Heidegger wrote about being "thrown" into existence in an abstract way, probably without realizing emotionally that this is the story of most people, including perhaps himself, but not of *all* people. There are some people, though not many, who have been raised protected and loved. Your mother lying on the sofa, filled with heroin, next to the highly intelligent little boy crying for attention whom she didn't see, represents to me the horror that you can *feel*; so many can't, and they have to endure illnesses instead.

MAY 2008

12 ◈ The Unfelt Pain

In my opinion, if you want "to get your pain off your mind," you become empty, suicidal, and alone, even with yourself. If you can feel your pain about having been treated so cruelly by your parents and siblings, you become vital, living with your history and moving into recovery. The *felt* pain doesn't last forever, but the *unfelt pain* of the little child you were insists on being heard. Try to listen to it.

18 ◈ Dependency as Adults?

Yes, I fully agree with your own answer. I would only add that pain and anger would also suggest that once you are on your own, with your true reliable enlightened witness within you, you might discover to your surprise that you are no longer as alone as before, and you might meet people (if not, perhaps, many) who think like you, who don't want to deny their past.

19 ℰ *Not Scared Anymore*

You write: "Thank you for giving me the courage to admit my pain. I am still working on my incest issues, but I am not scared anymore." It is feeling this pain and understanding, knowing the causes of this pain, that gives you the courage. It liberates you from the fear of things that *did* happen in the past but are no longer happening and thus should no longer be feared. In your short sentence you describe how effective therapy usually works.

23 ℰ *An Interview with Child Advocate Andrew Vachss*

I saw the interview. These are some of my thoughts about it: we will never be able to stop child abuse as long as we say: "I put the past behind me, I don't feel anger, have forgiven and forgotten and get on with my life." Saying that repeatedly never actually helps. Why? Because the endured abuse, if it is not worked out, drives the former victims to do the same with their children as long as they deny the pain and the anger, which the abuse left in their bodies. Our feelings may stay repressed, unconscious, for a long time, but they wake up when we become parents. Feeling and understanding the causes of our old pain does not mean that the pain and the anger will stay with us forever—quite the opposite is true. The felt anger and pain disappear with time, enabling us to love our children. It is the *unfelt*, avoided, and denied pain stored up in our bodies that drives us to repeat what has been done to us and to say, "Spanking didn't harm me—it was good for me and will thus also not harm my children." People who talk like this go on writing books on how we should spank babies early enough so that they learn to behave, never realizing what had been done to them so early in their lives.

24 ❧ Collective Unconscious

As children, we may potentially inherit the "shadows" of our parents, but as adults who dare to feel our truth and try to understand our feelings, we can liberate ourselves from these shadows by becoming conscious of them and rejecting them. If we no longer think that we must love a father who humiliated us, we become increasingly free of his coldness, his cruelty, and his confusion, and then nobody can make us imitate him. I also read the Web article you suggested. "Egophrenia" may be a good name for describing the madness of a dangerous politician, but playing with diagnoses does not explain anything about the *causes* of this madness. In my opinion, these causes are always hidden in the endured but denied cruelty of a childhood story. Unfortunately, as the article clearly shows, not only the Buddhist but also the Jungian "spirituality" helps us to stay blind toward the cruelty raging in the "best" families. I think, however, that there is no other way of liberating ourselves from lies and confusion than by becoming aware of our own suffering in childhood and by taking seriously the often tragic or even horrific reality of our fate. In denying this reality, as does the above-mentioned article by a well-known psychiatrist, we will fear during our whole life things that actually did happen in our past but will not happen again, simply because we no longer are children. But all mad and egophrenic dictators are driven by humiliations they endured as children; without consciously remembering them, they take revenge on scapegoats.

28 ⌾ *An Invitation to Honduras*

Unfortunately I am unable to travel to Honduras, but I have some ideas about how I can help you: All my flyers are free and will be soon available in Spanish on the Web site Natural Child. You can publish or distribute them among institutions that work with children or parents. You have nothing to pay for these texts. I think that if you can make my texts available to professionals who are still stuck in the traditional, destructive, abusive way of thinking, you have done more for children than if I came to Honduras. I wish you much success in your work against violence toward children and for more awareness and consciousness. This work is not easy indeed but absolutely necessary. Unfortunately, there are not many people who understand how we produce violence and that we could stop this production by becoming aware of its causes.

30 ⌾ *How to Make Up for Mistakes?*

The best you can do (for you and your child) is to work on your past, so that you come to understand where your anger comes from. You can tell your child that you are very sorry that you have spanked him; you didn't know then that a mother should never do this. Now, since you know that hitting children is wrong and dangerous, you promise him that you will never do it again. Don't ask him for forgiveness, for that would merely be a new burden. You should only inform him that you now know better, that you know of his suffering and regret what you have done. This is important, and you will see how positively it will work for both of you.

JUNE 2008

2 ᶜ *Panic Attacks and Dreams*

Exactly! You got it! It seems that your panic attacks can become
your guides; they can help you to take your needs seriously. Why
should you change and give up the job you obviously like? Because
somebody asked you to do so? Sometimes our body knows better than our mind what we actually want and need for the mind
may be busy with wanting to please. Congratulations on becoming
aware of what is going on.

3 ᶜ *How Can I Help Myself?*

You *are* already helping yourself by honestly acknowledging your
truth. This is the first unavoidable step, and it is always painful.
The body will guide you in making the next steps: you will become
angry and little by little you will be able to reclaim *your* life and
live it.

5 ᶜ *Paintings*

Your painting shows so much of what you already let us feel in
your letters: your strength in discovering your true authentic life
in spite of the terrible abuse you were suffering. It is a pleasure to
see you in your colorful and rich paintings. I think that what makes
us happy is not the word "artist"; it is, above all, the freedom to be
ourselves, to be able to freely express our feelings and to experience
pleasure when doing this.

5 ᴄ *Panics*

Your panic episodes are an indication of what happened to you.
Fortunately, you found a witness who *wants* to listen to your story
so you can work on it. This takes time, of course, but you will succeed because you want to know your truth.

12 ᴄ *Avoiding Pain*

Yes, you are right. They are used to it and are, in addition, used to
repressing pain so that they can avoid feeling it. They don't know
yet that the body will demand the price for this repression when
they become older.

20 ᴄ *Question About Parents*

Why should you not see your parents if you feel well being around
them? There are people who suffer a lot when they meet with their
parents, even when they talk to them only on the phone; they are
unable to talk frankly with their parents, must control every word
and are afraid of their exploding rage, which must remain hidden.
After such meetings they feel very sick. In *these* cases I ask people
why they think that they must visit and lie to their parents if they
feel so bad with them. But if it is not your case, why do you ask for
my opinion? Enjoy your good feelings and your good health.

21 ᴄ *Escaping an Obsessed Psychiatrist Father*

It is always very hard to deal with a sadist if you are dependent on
them. And as a child, you depend on your parents; you can't escape

them. Whatever you do, they succeed in making you suffer. Most people then feel, even as adults, that they are still dependent on their parents. And they *are*—as long as they wait for a change, for a miracle. They believe that a sadist will change because they think that they absolutely need a good father or mother. You are lucky in no longer believing this. To have a good attorney is the best way of communication in your situation. Congratulations. You have the courage to *see* the truth, and thanks to this sight you have the means to protect yourself.

28 & *Supernanny: Is She Good, or Is She the Best We Can Get?*

I agree with your observation. Can it be that these nannies learn some good things in their schools about how you have to talk to the child, etc., but that when they work with families they can't avoid the old patterns of their own upbringing and the way they were treated by their own parents, which stop them from being on the child's side? The same can happen to therapists, even if they had the best training.

28 & *Moving Beyond the Church's Complicity*

Why don't you write to the pope and ask him to listen to the cries of the millions of maltreated children who are daily brutally beaten by their religious parents to become obedient so that God will shine on them?

29 & *From a Reader of*
The Drama of the Gifted Child

It may be that there are already some therapists who use my method, but I don't know of it. However, you can check them by using my FAQ list, which you will find on my Web site under "Articles."

JULY 2008

3 & *Helping the Little Bloke*

Why don't you tell him that nobody has the right to hit and mistreat him, and that you will talk to his parents and tell them that what they are doing is a crime? It is your duty to protect this boy from the lies he has been taught and to tell him the truth. Otherwise so-called therapy is a farce.

3 & *Writing You from Spain*

I think that you clearly see that you must liberate yourself from the terrible pain. But I hope that one day you will be able to feel your (justified) anger and rage without feeling guilty. The pain is the expression of your taking upon yourself the guilt that others should feel. Even if they refuse to feel it, you should know that it is they who deserve the pain and not you. You were an innocent victim; don't forget that.

4 & *Confronting Our Parents*

You are asking me: "Do you think he might be able to [understand]? How can I encourage him? How can I reassure him?" My answer